A Judge in Auschwitz

A Judge in Auschwitz

Konrad Morgen's Crusade Against SS Corruption & 'Illegal' Murder

Kevin Prenger

Translated from Dutch by Arnold van Wulfften Palthe, 2020

Pen & Sword
MILITARY

First published in Great Britain in 2021 by
Pen & Sword Military
An imprint of
Pen & Sword Books Ltd
Yorkshire – Philadelphia

Copyright © Kevin Prenger 2021

ISBN 978 1 39901 876 0

Printed and bound in the UK by CPI Group (UK) Ltd,
Croydon, CR0 4YY.

Pen & Sword Books Limited incorporates the imprints of Atlas,
Archaeology, Aviation, Discovery, Family History, Fiction, History,
Maritime, Military, Military Classics, Politics, Select, Transport,
True Crime, Air World, Frontline Publishing, Leo Cooper, Remember
When, Seaforth Publishing, The Praetorian Press, Wharncliffe
Local History, Wharncliffe Transport, Wharncliffe True Crime
and White Owl.

For a complete list of Pen & Sword titles please contact

PEN & SWORD BOOKS LIMITED
47 Church Street, Barnsley, South Yorkshire, S70 2AS, England
E-mail: enquiries@pen-and-sword.co.uk
Website: www.pen-and-sword.co.uk

Or

PEN AND SWORD BOOKS
1950 Lawrence Rd, Havertown, PA 19083, USA
E-mail: Uspen-and-sword@casematepublishers.com
Website: www.penandswordbooks.com

Contents

Chapter I

Horrific Scenes

'Stacks, a few feet high, no humans anymore, just dry bones.' That was what Czech-born Holocaust survivor Jan Hartman saw in his mind's eye as he remembered the spring of 1945 in Buchenwald concentration camp. He saw how Russian prisoners-of-war in the camp were dying like flies. He had not yet seen so many corpses, even in Auschwitz where he had been interned earlier. He was more dead than alive himself though. He was what prisoners called *Muselmänner* among themselves, emaciated to the bones, hardly able to stand or walk from exhaustion. Buchenwald survivor John Chillag, also born a Czech, shared his fate. He was weakened and ill and had been staying in the sick bay before the liberation of the camp. According to him, the prisoners lying in the top bunks were so severely weakened they were unable to get down to eat or relieve themselves. He and his fellow inmates 'were just lying in those bunks, too weak to do anything and I couldn't have survived more than a day or two.'[1]

For people like Hartman and Chillag, the wait for the liberation of Buchenwald shouldn't have lasted any longer. The camp near Weimar was overcrowded after more than 10,000 weakened prisoners (mostly Jews) had arrived from Auschwitz and Gross-Rosen in January 1945, after exhausting marches and transports by train. At the end of March the camp housed 80,436 inmates. As American troops were approaching, inmates who were still fit enough were evacuated from Buchenwald on foot in deplorable conditions. About one third of the evacuated inmates perished during these death marches; exhausted and undernourished as they were, they could not keep up with the pace and were shot by their guards and left on the wayside. In the morning of 11 April the remaining inmates had seized control of the camp, and later that day the first Americans arrived. They found only 21,000 survivors. Jan Hartman remembers: 'One sunny day a well-dressed American soldier appeared at the far end of the barracks. That was liberation.' He and his brother spoke English and they bade welcome to their liberators. 'It was fantastic for them and it was fantastic for us.'[2] There was no question of a joyful atmosphere though. The scenes the Americans had witnessed in Buchenwald and previously in other concentration camps were just too gruesome.

Buchenwald was not the first concentration camp to be liberated by the Western Allies. That 'honour' fell to concentration camp Vught in the Netherlands where the Canadians only found empty barracks on 26 October 1944, after the inmates had been evacuated by the SS to other camps in Germany a month earlier. On 4 April 1945 the Americans saw before their very eyes the horrific scenes that are generally known today. In a satellite camp of Buchenwald, in the small town of Ohrdruf, troops of the 4th Armored Division of General George Patton's 3rd Army encountered dozens of corpses and numerous severely weakened inmates. The most gruesome sight was half burned corpses on pyres made of railway sleepers. Those were the remains of the efforts of the camp guards who had attempted to erase the traces of their crimes. They had opened the mass graves and tried to cremate all the corpses but failed to finish the job on time.

When Allied supreme commander Dwight Eisenhower and Patton paid a visit to camp Ohrdruf on 12 April they were shocked by what they saw. To reveal the crimes of the Nazis to the outside world, photographers and film crews were ordered to record the liberation of the German camps. They recorded how German civilians, ordered by Patton in Buchenwald, had to witness the crimes which had been committed under their very noses. With their mouths covered with handkerchiefs and tears in their eyes they walked past a stack of emaciated corpses. Spread out in front of them on a table lay pieces of tattooed human skin, human body parts in spirits, and a lamp shade allegedly made of human skin.

Throughout the war at least 56,000 inmates had perished in Buchenwald, but that was only the tip of the iceberg. The Allies encountered similar scenes in each concentration camp that was liberated in the spring of 1945. In Bergen-Belsen the number of corpses was so vast the British had to use a bulldozer to move all bodies into a communal grave to contain a further outbreak of typhoid fever. In the camps liberated by the western Allies, some 600,000 inmates had died. The numbers of deaths in camps liberated by the Soviets were even higher. In Auschwitz alone 1.1 million people had been killed, mostly Jews who had been murdered in gas chambers. The gruesome images of the liberated camps spread across the world and were shown at the Nuremberg trial where the surviving Nazi bigwigs had to atone for their crimes. The concentration and extermination camps of Nazi Germany became the symbol of Hitler's criminal regime. After the war hundreds upon hundreds of camp commanders and guards stood trial for the horrendous crimes they had committed.

A name that is missing from the long list of personnel from the camps who were brought to court after the war is that of Karl Otto Koch. He was in charge of camp Buchenwald from 1937 to 1941. It was not an Allied tribunal or a court in post-war Germany but an SS court that sentenced him to death. As late as 5 April 1945, as American troops were closing in on the camp, he was executed in Buchenwald by an SS firing squad. The case against Koch had started with a judicial investigation into corruption in Buchenwald conducted by SS judge Konrad Morgen. He was furious over the facts he discovered: along with some cronies, Koch had stolen from inmates and had abused and murdered them. For these reasons, he and a number of co-suspects, including his wife, notorious for her cruelty, were brought before a court of the SS.

Knowing everything we know today about Nazi Germany, it seems odd that Koch and his wife were charged with crimes which to us are synonymous with the regime in the German concentration camps, where theft, torture and murder were the order of the day. But Koch was not the only camp employee who had to deal with a judicial investigation by Konrad Morgen. After Buchenwald, Morgen launched investigations into crimes committed by employees in various large camps; even in Auschwitz, the location of the largest mass murder by the Nazis. Morgen took judicial steps against various notorious camp commanders; for example, against Amon Göth, the sadistic commander of camp Płaszów in Poland and against Rudolf Höss, who had been in charge of the assembly-line gassing of Jews in Auschwitz.

After the war Morgen described himself as a warrior for justice who had done everything he could to protect inmates against the violent excesses of their jailers. His judicial investigation into the crimes of employees of concentration camps and the ensuing prosecution of guards and commanders do not seem to fit into the history of the Third Reich where the most hideous crimes were part and parcel of government policy. Yet, his role was part of the history of Nazi Germany just like the henchmen he prosecuted.

Chapter II

Dragged Along by Hitler's Successes

According to Konrad Morgen, he had a warm and friendly face, the man who rode past in his shining Mercedes convertible on 19 May 1935 in the sun. Wearing his long leather coat and military cap, he made a strong impression. Morgen had seen him in real life in 1931 for the first time at a political meeting, but he knew his face mainly from the portraits which were displayed all over Germany. Back in 1931 he had only been a politician without authority, Adolf Hitler now was the unassailable leader of a Germany reborn. On that day in May 1935, he opened the umpteenth success of his tenure in office, the Autobahn from Frankfurt to Darmstadt. It was not yet two years ago that he had symbolically launched the construction of the highway by scooping up some sand.[1] The official inauguration was a masterpiece of propaganda: standing in his car with the swastika pennant flying on the right front fender, the *Führer* was driven past the crowds that had gathered along the road, all saluting ecstatically. Morgen was present that day along with other students to keep the public at bay. He was surprised by Hitler's sympathetic aura, the man who had restored Germany's pride in the '30s.

When Valentin Georg Konrad Morgen was born on 8 June 1909 in Frankfurt am Main, Hitler still was a non-descript homeless young man roaming about in Vienna. As Konrad's father was a train driver, his son had to climb the social ladder on his own. He did this very well. After graduating from *Oberrealschule* in 1929, he was a volunteer trainee at the Bankhaus Goldschmidt in his hometown. Subsequently he went to university and distanced himself from the bourgeois life of his parents. Morgen was interested in foreign languages and history and studied law at the universities of Frankfurt am Main, Rome and Berlin. He also studied at the Academy of International Law in The Hague and at the Institute for Global Economics and Shipping in Kiel, Germany. He lived in France as an exchange student. After successful completion of his studies, he was allowed to call himself Doctor of Law.[2]

Being specialized in international law, a bright career was on the horizon for him in Hitler's 'new Germany' where young academics like him had ample career opportunities, as long as they were loyal to national socialism and joined the party or some other connected organization. After the war Morgen claimed he had little interest in national socialism before Hitler rose to power. He considered himself a 'national-liberal'. In 1939 he had attended a meeting where Hitler was to speak, just because he wanted to hear him for once. He was disillusioned by the speech as he felt Hitler was continuously 'talking about himself' and made promises without indicating how to fulfill them. Morgen did not feel like an enemy of the party yet but he did not expect much of national socialism either.[3] His father was equally critical of national socialism, but not his mother: 'She let herself be dragged along by all the flag waving, the speeches and the singing and marching columns. She hoped that with Hitler, a major turning point had emerged.'[4]

It was not long after Hitler's appointment to *Reichskanzler* (chancellor) in January 1933 however, that Konrad Morgen joined the ranks of the National Socialists. On 1 March 1933 he became a member of the *Allgemeine-SS*,[5] the civil branch from which men were recruited for the SS, *Sicherheitsdienst* (SD), and other branches of Himmler's SS. Based on his education and his sturdy build, he was immediately appointed *SS-Rottenführer*. After the war he claimed he had never really been a member of the *Allgemeine-SS* but just a *Bewerber* (candidate). This is contradicted however by having had a membership number as well as the rank of *SS-Rottenführer*, both impossible for candidates.[6] Morgen also claimed his enrollment in the *Allgemeine-SS* had not been voluntary but compulsory. According to his own words, he had become a member in 1933 of the *Reichskuratorium für Jugendertüchtigung*, an organization that taught German youngsters 'discipline, orderliness, companionship and … willingness to sacrifice in favour of the community by means of sports'.[7] After the seizure of power, the nature of this organization changed because the SA and SS began to interfere. Morgen declared: 'We had a new sports coach and we heard this instructor was a former officer, now dressed in civilian garb. The sport and the gymnastic exercises gradually took on the nature of preliminary military exercises, and ultimately they evolved into military drill.' On a certain day, according to him, an inspection was held and the younger children were told that from that moment on they would be members of the SA while the older children heard that they were to be incorporated in the *Allgemeine-SS*. That is, in his words, how Morgen joined the SS.[8]

Whether or not his enrollment in the *Allgemeine-SS* proceeded in the way Morgen claims cannot be verified. Admittedly the *Reichskuratorium für Jugendertüchtigung* was incorporated in the SA after the seizure of power and many members ultimately ended up in the SS, but in principle membership of the SS was voluntarily. After all, the organization was meant as an elite organization to which initially only men meeting strict requirements were admitted. Hence it cannot be excluded that Morgen opted to join the SS of his own free will. The elite organization appealed to young well-educated men in particular. While the brownshirts of the SA were associated with street fights and brawls in beer halls, the blackshirts of the SS were considered disciplined representatives of the new regime. It can however be concluded from the fact that Morgen retained the same rank until 1939 that he had not been overly active and did not play a leading role in the *Allgemeine-SS*.[9]

On 1 April 1933, a month after he had joined the SS, Morgen became member number 2,536,236 of the NSDAP.[10] He did so on the advice of his parents, so he said. Another reason for his membership he mentioned after the war was that it was necessary for continuing his study as he was in his sixth semester. 'At Frankfurt university, one had to prove to be a member of the party and one of its branches,' he said.[11] Membership was also mandatory for entering public service. He claimed not to have participated in activities of the party. He was a member of the NSDStB, the Nazi Student Union, and the *NS-Rechtswahrenbund* (Union of Nazi Lawyers) though. He appears to have been one of the many opportunists who joined the party only after it had taken power. The influx of new members was so big that the party decided to declare a *numerus clausus* in May 1933, afraid as it was that the movement would be flooded with people not really loyal to national socialism. People like Morgen who had enrolled in the NSDAP shortly before the ban were mockingly called *Märzgefallenen* (victims of March) by the veterans of the party, an ironic reference to the victims of the March uprisings of 1848 in Vienna and Berlin and the Kapp-Putsch of March 1920.

Morgen also claimed to have remained critical of Hitler after the seizure of power. After the demise of *Reichspräsident* Paul von Hindenburg on 2 August 1934, the German population was called upon to vote for an extension of Hitler's authority: the functions of *Reichspräsident* and *Reichskanzler* were to be united. This meant that Hitler would no longer just be the leader of the party and the government but head of state and commander-in-chief of the armed forces as well. This gave him far reaching powers, as the state president was inviolable and could impose measures by emergency decree. According to official numbers, 89.9 per cent[12] of the voters voted in favour of Hitler's appointment to *Führer* and state chancellor, but Morgen did not. The unification of the two highest functions in the state 'went right against his judicial conviction'. He refused to vote in favour of Hitler's extension of power, but did not dare to vote against it either, let alone express his views openly. He was afraid that if he did so, 'something terrible' would happen to him. 'As I did not want to commit suicide,' he argued with slightly dramatic exaggeration, 'I told myself: if you don't vote, you don't have to go against your conviction.'[13] The local branch of the party reprimanded him on his refusal to vote. 'Finally, I had been demasked,'[14] he declared. A charge was brought against him to have him excluded from the party, but thanks to the help of unnamed SS men, this was prevented.

Morgen may have joined the party for opportunistic reasons and he may have had judicial objections to Hitler's extension of power, nonetheless he was dragged along in the wake of the many successes Hitler had achieved during the 30s, like so many millions of other Germans. After the war Morgen declared he had got used to political parties not fulfilling their promises and the National Socialist party did just that. He had friends and acquaintances who had been unemployed for five to eight years and still nobody had found a solution. As 'Germans are born to work,' he considered the massive unemployment during the Weimar period a serious problem.[15] Hitler promised, according to Morgen, 'work and bread on the shelf for the millions of unemployed who were starving, and he actually succeeded although nobody had deemed it possible. Even in a relatively short time! All those people who had just existed until that time without any future could see with their own eyes that their life had meaning again and they had a duty – by working you could feed and support your family again instead of living on charity.'[16]

On his way to university Morgen always passed an engine plant which before the change of power had always been a mess and working conditions poor. After Hitler had taken power, Morgen saw the changes: everything was tidied up, flowers had been planted and benches put up where workers could have their smoke. Morgen also praised the cheap holidays for workers that were organized by the National Socialist organization *Kraft durch Freude* (strength through joy). In addition he highly praised Hitler's courage for ordering the construction of the Autobahn (highways), an enterprise nobody, in his opinion, had dared to undertake because of the immense cost. The positive changes he experienced in Germany made him change his mind about Hitler's politics. He was neither a fanatical devotee of Hitler, nor was he an opponent of the Nazis.

There are however no indications that he felt attracted to the anti-Semitism of the party, nor is there irrefutable evidence showing that he distanced himself from it. After the war he declared that 'anti-Semitism was just one of those points in the programme that evoked general aversion and against which you resisted in some sense'. But he did not feel uneasy. 'You said – to yourself – there has never been a party in power that has entirely fulfilled its programme. In other words, many allegedly iron-clad principles get snowed under or get toned down. After all, the situation was not so bad as it seemed.'[17]

Such an attitude was not uncommon; after the war, other former party members declared they had also been gripped by Hitler's promises to restore Germany to a forceful and healthy nation and that rabid anti-Semitism seemed something temporary to them which would blow over one day. After the public protests against the Jews in the spring of 1933, with the anti-Jewish boycott of April as the lowest point, during the following years massive and public protests against Jews did not occur. It culminated into a violent escalation on '*Kristallnacht*' – 9 and 10 November 1938 – when all over Germany synagogues went up in flames and Jewish shops and homes were demolished. During the years in between, anti-Semitism was not absent but became visible through discriminating laws, in particular the Nuremberg racial laws of September 1935 forbidding Jews to marry and have sexual relations with non-Jews. There were no protests against such expressions of anti-Semitism: many Germans felt it necessary that measures be taken to lessen Jewish influence on society, as long as it was done in a 'civilized' manner.

Chapter III

Pacifist or Warrior?

Konrad Morgen claimed to have been mistaken not only about Hitler's anti-Semitism but in his hunger for war as well. In the witness box during the Nuremburg trial he was asked whether he knew anything about Hitler's plans for war when he joined the SS. He replied he had written a book in 1936 entitled *Kriegspropaganda und Kriegsverhütung* (war propaganda and prevention of war). He declared: 'This book, at a time when war was threatening, showed ways and means to prevent war and to forestall the incitement to hostility between nations. The book was examined by the Party and published. Therefore, I could not suppose that the SS or the policy of the Reich Government was directed toward war.'[1] The book was published by Noske in Leipzig. According to the review by the party, the book had 'a purely scientific value but no political potential',[2] Morgen claimed during his denazification trial in Ludwigsburg in 1948. The book did not directly incite to war, but the message was far from pacifistic. Morgen did distance himself from the antimilitaristic-pacifist propaganda that, in his words, 'applies exactly the same methods as the actual war propaganda'. He continued:

'It appeals to the same destructive passions, motives and instincts. This only occurs with a negative omen. Against war!

Just as war propaganda arouses hatred against foreign opponents, so antimilitaristic-pacifist propaganda arouses hatred against its own citizens. (The enemy stands on the right!) Just as war propaganda reports alleged atrocities, so antimilitaristic-pacifist propaganda holds its own (wage slavery, tenement housing distress, working soldiers to death). Just as war propaganda fills the nation with distrust of foreign governments, so antimilitaristic-pacifist propaganda directs its distrust at the national government (a regime of landowners and industrialists). Just as war propaganda denigrates the foreign enemy, so the method of the antimilitaristic-pacifistic propaganda idolizes foreign countries and sullies the Fatherland.'[3]

While expressing his aversion to pacifistic propaganda, Morgen spoke highly about national socialism in his book. It appears he seriously believed that Hitler was not bent on war. 'The National Socialist disassociation from war founded on world-view is laid down. It is therefore independent of all exterior circumstances and is valid as long as national socialism exists.'[4] The battle that national socialism should wage was, in his view, one without weapons but one of diligent labour:

> 'Our young men are toiling and moiling on their own soil in the *Arbeitsdienst*. By cultivating and draining land and by irrigation, internal colonization of large tracts of land is achieved without loss of blood and the rattling of swords. Our scientific ingenuity replaces essential raw materials our poor soil denies us and those other powers, that have distributed the earth among themselves, provide us with insufficiently. SA and SS are ready to teach them soldierly disposition and physical productivity, thereby making any new *Stahlbad* (war) redundant. The large *Kraft durch Freude* organization provides even the poorest and lowest classed *Volksgenossen* with the opportunity to take in the highest cultural heritage and see the beauties of the world with their own eyes.
>
> That is our fight against poverty, ignorance, our own failures and the darkness of our souls. That is our struggle for a better standard of living, for the soul of our people, for a higher liberation of humanity.
>
> That is our war! our perennial war as proclaimed by our *Führer*. This war does not benefit the rich but in particular the poor. Its sacrifices will not be demanded from the unpropertied but from the rich. This heroism threatens no one.'[5]

According to American professor Randall Bytwerk, an expert on Nazi propaganda, the quotations clearly show that the book has been written from a Nazi perspective. However, he calls the 'Nazi grade' of the book 'relatively limited'. Bytwerk notes for instance that the fanatic master of propaganda Joseph Goebbels is never quoted. 'He quotes extensively from one of Hitler's speeches but quotes no fragments from *Mein Kampf* about propaganda. The majority of the quotes were taken from scientific publications, most of them from outside Germany.'

The claim Morgen made after 1945 about not having been a Nazi is, according to Bytwerk, not supported by the text in the book.[6] German professor of journalism Kurt Koszyk places the book in a wider perspective. In his opinion it is one of the 'numerous [German] publications ... dealing with the scope of Allied propaganda in order to find excuses for Germany's defeat in the First World War.' He thinks such publications about propaganda have a propagandistic nature of their own.[7] Morgen may have been more moderate than Goebbels and other well-known Nazi-propagandists, but in his book he portrayed himself as a follower of national-socialism. Although he did not use belligerent language, it was not pacifistic either.

That Morgen had not been a pacifist also becomes clear from what he said during a post-war interview about Hitler's successes in the war against Poland and France. He referred to a discussion he had held during the war with an acquaintance of his father. The man had fought in the First World War and told him that the battle of Verdun had claimed the lives of 1.2 million Germans[8] 'and Hitler achieved that in one afternoon'. (Verdun was captured on 15 June 1940.) Morgen praised the German successes in the war which convinced him once again he had underestimated Hitler's political ability prior to 1933.[9]

In Morgen's personal life before the war there also has been some talk about an occurrence which shows that in principle he was not against violence. It is about a conflict he had with the economist Karl Julius Speck in 1938. On 5 March the two had an argument. Morgen had felt so insulted that he had sent a letter on 8 March to *SS-Hauptsturmführer* Stroh of the arbitration committee of the SS region which included Frankfurt am Main. In it he requested an *Ehrenverfahren* be opened, a case to defend his honour.[10] Such trials were held by the SS to settle personal conflicts between its members. Ultimately it could be decided that a member of the SS was obliged to 'defend his honour by force of arms'. This implied a duel had to be held. Himmler preferred though that arguments be settled without the rattling of arms and from 1943 onwards these kinds of 'duels' would in principle be forbidden 'for the duration of the war'.[11]

In his letter to *SS-Hauptsturmführer* Stroh, Morgen described the incident. It had taken place in the home of a friend where he and Karl Julius Speck were guests. The two men did not know each other well but they had met one another occasionally in and around the court hall in Frankfurt where at that time Morgen was being prepared for the function of judge. The two men engaged in a vicious argument. Morgen charged Speck with having physically threatened him and having spoken to him in a condescending way. 'If I had as little brain in my head as you have, I would feel sorry,' he claimed Speck said. 'This insult was a very grave one', so Morgen said. As he was a guest in the house of a friend, he had no wish to deepen the argument any further so he had left the house without speaking a further word.

First thing next day Morgen informed his local commander, *SS-Oberscharführer* Dietz, that he wished to defend his honour by force of arms. Over the next two days Dietz had attempted to forward the request to Speck, but on both days he did not find him at home. That was the reason why Morgen had sent his letter to *SS-Hauptsturmführer* Stroh. In it he emphasized that as far as he was concerned Speck was not a member of the SS, and that as rumour had it he had been ousted from the party for not having paid his membership fee regularly. Morgen could not pass judgment whether Speck 'was a man of National Socialist honour'. On 11 March 1938, *SS-Hauptsturmführer* Stroh sent a letter to Speck offering the choice between settling the argument by mutual agreement or having it brought to court according to the rules of the SS. It could have been quite intimidating for Speck to receive such a letter from the SS with that kind of content. On 16 March 1938 he replied he would prefer a mutual agreement provided Morgen would take back his words. The next day Stroh demanded both opponents meet him on 20 March. After this meeting had taken place, Morgen sent a reply in writing to Stroh, saying he would, on his suggestion, abstain from a duel. He did demand however that Speck would apologize in writing. Morgen had even drafted the apologies for his opponent. 'I regret my conduct towards Dr Konrad Morgen during the incident on 5 March in the home of Mr Wilhelm Müller and take back my insulting remarks with deepest regret.'

Apologies followed on 12 April. Both opponents were again summoned by Stroh. The declaration Morgen had drafted was copied by Speck almost verbatim but he added he had been drinking alcohol and had become irritated by certain questions from Morgen and in this mood had made insulting remarks. Morgen accepted his apologies and declared he had had no malicious intent with his remarks. That was the end of that.

On 5 May Stroh reported to the leader of his SS district, *SS-Oberführer* Kurt Brasack, that the issue had been solved by mutual agreement.[12] Hence a duel did not materialize, but the fact that Morgen had wished to settle an apparently minor conflict with it makes one suspect he felt more at home within the ranks of the violent Nazi movement than he had made it appear after the war. In those days, fencing duels were common among conservative students and many an SS face was marred by scars from their period as students.

In 1939 Morgen clashed with a colleague again. That year he was employed as lawyer and judge on the *Landesgericht* (federal court) in Stettin until war broke out. The conflict occurred in the court room where he, as assistant examiner, was involved in a case against a pedagogue. It is unclear why the man stood trial. According to Morgen, the defendant had 'frequent problems with the Hitler Youth' and would lose his pension if convicted. Morgen stated that the defendant did not get a fair trial. 'The president of the court was notorious,' Morgen declared after the war during his denazification trial. 'He conducted the case in such a way that the verdict guilty was inevitable.' When Morgen objected, his right to ask questions was denied and the hearing was aborted. Morgen stood firmly by his judicial principles and refused to take part in the proceedings any longer. 'Then I was out on the street, from one moment to the next,' he declared.[13] On 1 April 1939 he was fired for disciplinary reasons. After the war he used his dismissal as proof of his critical attitude towards the regime. He did find a new job, though with a National Socialist organization. He started work as legal advisor for the *Deutsches Arbeitsfront*, the national worker's organization. Among other things, as their lawyer he represented workers in legal cases.[14]

Chapter IV

The Dual State

After the outbreak of war on 1 September 1939, Konrad Morgen was drafted into the *Waffen-SS*, the military branch of the SS. He took basic military training in the *Ersatz-Bataillon-Ost* in Breslau (today Wrocław in Poland) and subsequently served as officer for social and judicial matters on the regimental staff of 12. *SS-Regiment* in Posen (Poznań). His unit did not see active service at the front. In October 1940 he was promoted to *SS-Hauptscharführer*. In the same month he was transferred to the *Hauptamt SS-Gericht* as deputy judge. He was trained, attended sessions and familiarized himself with military law.[1] The *Hauptamt SS-Gericht* was one of the future twelve main departments of the SS. The department dealt with judicial matters within the SS, including persecuting and sentencing members of the SS who had been charged with transgressions or crimes while on duty. For instance this could include theft, corruption and insubordination. Murdering and torturing inmates of concentration camps could also be considered a crime while at the same time the SS was responsible for the extermination of the Jews. Murder and torture were the order of the day in the camps managed by the organization.

This contradiction was a result of the form of government in the Third Reich. The German-Jewish political scientist Ernst Fraenkel (1898–1975), who fled his country in 1938, described it in his book entitled *The Dual State* (1941). On the one hand, it consisted of the *Normenstaat* ('normative state') bound by laws and measures and represented by formal departments like in every modern state, such as the ministerial departments, the judicial apparatus, police and the penal system. On the other, he distinguished a *Massnahmenstaat* ('prerogative state') consisting of organizations and agencies not bound to laws and drawing their legitimacy from Hitler's authority. Hitler's power as *Führer* was 'total and all encompassing, which includes all means available to the state', as emphasized by the National Socialist constitution lawyer Ernst

Rudolph Huber in 1939. 'The authority of the *Führer* is not subject to any limiting or controlling power; it is not contained by autonomous private domains and closely guarded individual rights; it is free and independent, decisive and unbound.'[2] While public servants, police officers and judges remained bound to largely the same laws and regulations that had already been in force during the Weimar period (1918–33), now organizations and agencies emerged within the Third Reich that were accountable to Hitler only and were authorized, on his orders, to violate existing laws and measures. The clearest example of such an organization was the SS.

The SS, initially established as Hitler's personal bodyguard, was increasingly deployed to do the dirty work after January 1933. In the spring of 1934, Hitler decided to get rid of Ernst Röhm and other high-ranking members of the *Sturmabteilung* (SA) as the brownshirts became too great a threat to his authority. He was partially incited to this action by a fake rumour to the effect that Röhm was preparing a coup. It had been Reinhard Heydrich, chief of the *Sicherheitsdienst*, who had planted this rumour, basing it on fabricated evidence. Heydrich was supported by his boss, Heinrich Himmler, and Nazi bigwigs like Hermann Göring and Joseph Goebbels were only too eager to have their rival for power eliminated. Moreover, the leadership of the *Reichswehr* (German army) urged Hitler and his conservative political cronies to curtail the power of the SA. It was feared that it would push the National Socialist revolution on further and that the SA would grow into a party army that would outdo the *Reichswehr*. Hitler opted for a drastic solution to the problem. From 30 June to 2 July at least eighty-five prominent people, including Röhm and other SA leaders, were murdered on his orders. Many more people were arrested; Göring alone ordered the arrest of over 1,000 persons.[3] The bloody night of 30 June to 1 July went down in history as the Night of the Long Knives. It was the SS that was responsible for the cruel murders. According to the laws of the *Normenstaat*, murder was a crime, but according to the superior norms of the *Massnahmenstaat* it was legitimate, as Hitler, being the infallible head of state, had given the order.

Another example of how the SS could ignore the laws of the *Normenstaat* was the judicial instrument euphemistically called *Schutzhaft* (protective custody). The day after the fire of the *Reichstag* on 27 February 1933, the Nazi government issued the emergency law '*zur Schutzung des Volkes und des Staates*' (protection of population and state). Although the Dutch communist Marinus van der Lubbe was the only one to be convicted for having set fire to the government building, the Nazis assumed it was a communist plot against the state. Pursuant to this emergency law, personal freedoms as guaranteed under the Weimar constitution, like freedom of the press and of speech, were suspended. Communists as well as social-democrats, labour union leaders and leftist intellectuals were rounded up by the SA and the SS in droves and taken into *Schutzhaft* in improvised prisons and camps. This meant they would be detained indefinitely without any kind of trial with the argument that their safety outside captivity could no longer be guaranteed. In reality the measure was applied to remove would-be opponents to the regime from society for a few weeks or even for years. In March and April 1933 an estimated 40,000 to 50,000 opponents were taken into 'protective custody'.[4] The possibility to take people into protective custody remained throughout the entire Nazi period. Until the end of the war, political opponents accounted for a fair share of the inmates in the concentration camps.

And yet the SS itself was not entirely free from judicial prosecution. In 1933, German justice still had some authority over the hastily established concentration camps, the so called *Frühe Konzentrationslager* (preliminary camps). These camps were located for instance in abandoned factory buildings, cellars and old schools. They were poorly managed and hardly monitored. Guards of the SA and the SS often committed serious forms of torture on prisoners, which often led to their deaths. One of the most notorious camps was located in the shipyard of AG Vulcan in Stettin (today Szczecin in Poland). In February 1934 this camp was closed by order of the public prosecutor. Some members of the SA and SS were sentenced to long prison terms[5] for having instigated the torture of prisoners. On 22 March 1933 the first official concentration camp was established in Dachau near Munich. Initially conditions did not differ from those in most of the early camps. The camp commander, *SS-Hauptsturmführer* Hilmar Wäckerle, was a cruel and incompetent leader who gave his guards a free hand to vent their aggression on inmates. In June 1933 the public prosecutor in Bavaria charged him, the camp physician and another member of the staff with complicity to the assassination of four prisoners.[6] Himmler decided to fire the camp commander and on 26 June 1933 he replaced him with Theodor Eicke.

Eicke, born 17 October 1892 in Hampont, Alsace-Lorraine, was a former police officer and former security agent in the chemical concern of IG Farben. He had been a member of the NSDAP since 1928 and had enrolled in the SS in 1929. In the early 30s he was sentenced for having planned attacks on political opponents of the Nazis in Bavaria, but he evaded punishment by escaping to Italy where he ran a camp for fugitives on behalf of the Fascist government. After the seizure of power by the Nazi party he returned to Germany. Following a serious quarrel with a *Gauleiter* which ran completely out of hand he ended up in a psychiatric hospital. He was released in June 1933 by Himmler to set things straight in Dachau. During his tenure as camp commander, he instigated a policy that was eventually introduced in all concentration camps.

Eicke was the 'inventor' of the 'Disciplinary and penal measures for the prison camp' and the 'Instructions for companions and guards of prisoners'. In this way he created order in the chaos and arbitrariness that had been prevalent in the camps until then. Although guards were now bound to rules, this did not mean that torturing and killing of prisoners were things of the past. On the contrary: a prisoner who 'talks about politics with seditious intent', so Eicke's instructions read, 'gathers with others or spreads horror propaganda of the enemy, shall be hanged according to revolutionary justice; he who attacks a guard, disobeys an order or makes himself guilty of mutiny in any other way shall be shot out of hand or hanged later.' Hard labour, beating with sticks or being tied to a tree for hours on end were accepted forms of punishment, in addition to lighter penalties such as not receiving or sending mail.[7] In this way legitimacy was lent to actions by guards that had still been punishable in the Republic of Weimar. Himmler was very pleased about the way Eicke had reorganized the concentration camp in Dachau, and on 4 July 1934 he promoted him to *Inspektor der Konzentrationslager*. Eicke remodelled the entire camp system, which was now under full control of the SS. To the outside world, the camps were presented as well-organized institutions where inmates were being re-educated to become obedient citizens once more, harshly but according to strict rules. In this way, accusations from outside against SS guards and the camp system were avoided.

Chapter V

Justice Within the SS

In the years before the war, the influence of the SS increased steadily. On 17 June 1936 Himmler was appointed chief of the German police, and the German police system was integrated into the SS organization. With the police being part of Himmler's imperium of power and the replacement of uncooperative associates of justice by National Socialist prosecutors and judges, the *Normenstaat* was hardly able to impose restrictions on the SS. The authority of the SS in Germany could hardly be challenged, but when members of the SS were serving at the front during the invasion of Poland in September 1939, protests against their conduct began to emerge from the *Wehrmacht* nonetheless. These complaints mainly pertained to the *Einsatzgruppen*, the specially formed SS units tasked with, among other things, executing members of the Polish intelligentsia and Jews. *Wehrmacht* commanders even attempted to persecute SS members for their crimes during the Polish campaign. For instance, *General der Artillerie* Georg von Küchler, commander of *3. Armee*, ordered the disarmament and arrest of a police unit which, as part of *Einsatzgruppe V*, had murdered Jews and set fire to their homes. He took members of an SS regiment to court-martial for having herded fifty Jews into a synagogue and subsequently having executed them without any immediate cause.[1] An officer of the *Geheime Feldpolizei* and a soldier of the SS would have been sentenced to nine and three years respectively for their role in the crime mentioned above.[2]

To prevent civil courts and military tribunals of the *Wehrmacht* intervening in the prosecution of members of the SS, Hitler placed the police as well as the SS under *Sondergerichtsbarkeit* (special jurisdiction). From then on, the SS took the adjudgment of its members entirely in its own hands. Initially this applied only to full-time officials employed by the SS, men of the *SS-Verfügungstruppe* (the forerunner of the *Waffen-SS*), members of the *Totenkopfverbände* (guards in the concentration camps), students of the *Junkerschulen* (schools for officers) and members of police units in 'special service'. Later on it encompassed the entire SS and police organization. SS members who committed violations and crimes while on duty were prosecuted by regional *SS- und Polizeigerichte* (SS and police courts) subordinate to the *Hauptamt SS-Gericht*. These courts were located in Germany as well as in occupied territory. Mobile courts were part of every major division of the *Waffen-SS*. The highest SS and police court (comparable to a supreme court) was situated in Munich and handled charges against members of the SS concerning espionage and treason, attacks directed at the *Führer*, and sabotage. Charges against persons in the rank of *SS-Brigadeführer* and higher were also dealt with by this court in Munich.

The judicial system of the SS was based on military legislation within the *Wehrmacht*. The highest judicial authority was in the hands of so-called *Gerichtsherren*. They were not the judges adjudging the defendants but gave orders to start a criminal investigation, drafted the indictment, appointed the judges and confirmed or reversed verdicts. Formally, Hitler and Himmler acted as *Gerichtsherren* within the SS, although in practice this responsibility was usually entrusted to the superiors of the defendant: chiefs of SS main offices, the *Höhere SS- und Polizeiführer*, or the divisional commanders of the *Waffen-SS*. The trials were conducted by special *SS Richter*, special judges like Konrad Morgen; university graduates employed by the *Hauptamt SS-Gericht*. Just as in military courts, professional judges were assisted during proceedings by *Beisitzer* (lay judges).[3] At least one of those lay judges had to be of the same rank as the defendant and at the same time a higher ranking officer had to sit in the court.[4] A verdict by an *SS- und Polizeigericht* was only binding after it had been ratified by a *Gerichtsherr*. They were authorized to postpone prison sentences until after the war and could place convicts in the *Straflager der SS- und Polizei* (penal camp) in Dachau. They could also transfer convicts to a *Bewahrungseinheit* (penal battalion) of the *Waffen-SS* where they had to do dangerous work like clearing minefields and where they could be granted a safe pardon after having displayed courage.

That the judicial apparatus of the SS was up to its job is shown by the following figures: in the first quarter of 1943, 2,764 cases appeared before *SS- und Polizeigerichte*, resulting in 69 death penalties and over 2,000 prison terms.[5] It goes without saying that jurisdiction within the SS was based on National Socialist ideology. The American historian James J.

Weingartner declared that 'accordingly, the SS Judge was expected to conduct himself in a manner fundamentally different from that of the traditional fighter and educator to whom principle took precedence over paragraph. Not only were his decisions expected to directly further the ideological aims of the movement, but also to serve as precepts supplementing the ideological indoctrination of SS members.'[6]

Weingartner mentions an example to substantiate his claim. It is a case against two members of the *Waffen-SS* who were indicted for having had sexual contact with a black prostitute in a brothel in France. Although the *Gesetz zum Schutze des Deutschen Blutes und der Deutschen Ehre* from 1935 (Law to protect German blood and German honour) only explicitly forbade Germans or people of 'related blood' from having extramarital relationships with Jews, these two men nevertheless were dishonorably discharged and sentenced to two years imprisonment. The judge obviously considered sexual contact with a black woman just as damaging to German blood as with a Jewess.[7] Numerous cases though had nothing to do with ideology and pertained to violations and crimes common to any regular armed force, like absence without official leave and disobedience of orders. Non-military crimes such as maltreatment, murder, drunkenness and rape were penalized by *SS- und Polizeigerichte* as well, as were homosexual contacts.

The majority of cases handled by the *SS- und Polizeigerichte* were property crimes, such as material damage and theft. Out of all people sentenced by these courts in 1942, 42 per cent were pronounced guilty of such crimes.[8] Himmler saw it as an important virtue that his men kept their hands off other people's property. In November 1936 he issued an ordinance about the 'sanctity of ownership' in which he ordered that from then on no locks were to be placed on the lockers in the quarters of his SS men.[9] SS men should be able to trust each other and even the theft of a cigarette was below their dignity. They were also to keep their hands off the properties of the Jews who were murdered in the extermination camps; the SS leader emphasized this in his notorious speech to his officers in Posen (Poznań) on 4 October 1943. On that occasion he declared:

'The wealth they possessed we took from them. I gave a strict order, which has been carried out by *SS-Obergruppenführer* Pohl, that this wealth will of course be turned over to the Reich in its entirety. We have taken none of it for ourselves. Individuals who have erred will be punished in accordance with the order given by me at the start, threatening that anyone who takes as much as a single Mark of this money is a dead man. A number of SS men – they are not very many – committed this offence, and they shall die. There will be no mercy. We had the moral right, we had the duty towards our people, to destroy this people that wanted to destroy us. But we do not have the right to enrich ourselves by so much as a fur, as a watch, by one Mark or a cigarette or anything else. We do not want, in the end, because we destroyed a bacillus, to be infected by this bacillus and to die.'[10]

Himmler's ideal image of his men was far removed from reality though. Just like in other ranks of the Third Reich, many within the SS were guilty of self-enrichment. Poland in particular, subjected as it was to a regime of terror, was a beehive of corruption. In the concentration and extermination camps located there, many SS men could not keep their hands off possessions taken away from inmates and murdered Jews. But just like in camps in Germany and countries other than Poland, camp commanders and guards did not behave themselves as expected. The instructions, introduced by Eicke, could not prevent camp personnel from torturing and murdering inmates on their own initiative and without permission from their superiors.

Like no one else, Morgen gained insight into the rotten and corrupted system of the SS. Although specialized in international law, as an SS judge he occupied himself by mainly prosecuting SS men who were guilty of corruption and theft. He did so initially in the *Generalgouvernement* (General Government) in Poland but later on he was tasked with conducting criminal research in concentration camps in Germany and elsewhere.

Chapter VI

In the General Government

After the Germans had conquered Poland in September 1939, the country was partitioned: the west was annexed by Germany, the centre became the General Government and the eastern part was occupied by the Russians. The General Government was the largest part and initially consisted of four districts: the Warsaw, Radom, Krakow and Lublin districts. Following the German invasion of the Soviet Union in June 1941, eastern Galicia was added as the fifth district and named the Lviv district. Although the General Government was not an official part of the German Empire, it was under German rule. This force of occupation was headed by Governor-General Hans Frank.

Born 23 May 1900 in Karlsruhe, this lawyer had joined the NSDAP as early as 1923, and in the years before the seizure of power he had proved himself in court to be a talented defender of party members, including Hitler. After the seizure of power by the Nazis, the party lawyer was Secretary of Justice in Bavaria from 1933 to 1934 and he occupied himself equalizing the judicial apparatus of the federal states. From 25 October 1939 until the General Government was captured by the Red Army in January 1945, he was the governor there. He imagined himself as a king: he took official residence in Wawel Castle in Krakow, during the Middle Ages the residence of the Kings of Poland. Postage stamps bore his effigy and the territory he ruled was jokingly called 'Frank-reich' (reich also means rich). Frank and his wife were notorious for their boundless rapacity: they stole antique furniture, works of art, jewelry and other valuables from everyone everywhere. The General Government with its governor as role model evolved into a beehive of corruption.

Within the SS and police force in the General Government, which was supervised by the *Höhere SS- und Polizeiführer* and *SS-Obergruppenführer* Friedrich Wilhelm Krüger from 1939 until 1943, there was excessive self-enrichment as well. An SS judge had plenty of work to do here. After a period of orientation in Munich, Morgen was transferred to the

SS- und Polizeigericht in Krakow in January 1941 as assistant judge in the capital of the General Government and home town of Hans Frank. 1 March 1941 saw him promoted to *SS-Untersturmführer* there.[1] Morgen investigated and found out that camp commander Leckebusch ran a clandestine casino in a village in Krakow. Morgen had the place occupied and had Leckebusch's private home searched. As investigative judge, he handled a few cases. One of them was in an SS training camp in Debica in southern Poland. It had come to his attention that many criminal cases were reported from there. It was discovered that the camp commander had sent presents to the *Höhere SS- und Polizeiführer*, probably intending to blackmail him. Most of the SS men working in the camp were arrested. Leckebusch escaped arrest by committing suicide.[2]

A few months after being commissioned in Krakow, Morgen unearthed another corruption scandal in a warehouse of the SS. He had the manager of the warehouse, *SS-Hauptsturmführer* Dr Georg von Sauberzweig, arrested, along with his forty-strong staff on suspicion of serious economic crimes.[3] Von Sauberzweig had sold properties stolen from Poles and had shared the profit with some subordinate cronies. Despite his service record as a Nazi party veteran, he was subpoenaed by the *SS- und Polizeigericht* in Warsaw. On 18 August 1941 the court pronounced him guilty of 'continuous bribery of public servants and serious embezzlement'. He was sentenced to death by firing squad. Being a personal protégé of Oswald Pohl, chief of the *SS-Wirtschafts und Verwaltingshauptamt* – responsible for administrative and economic affairs within the SS – was no help to him, nor was a plea for pardon to Hitler. On 9 March 1942 the verdict was ratified by the *Führer* and the sentence was carried out on 9 April 1942.[4]

The case against Von Sauberzweig led Morgen onto the trail of another corrupt SS officer. Before his arrest, Von Sauberzweig had managed to alert his wife that she had to inform *SS-Standartenführer* Fegelein of his arrest immediately. Hermann Fegelein (1906–45) joined the *Allgemeine-SS* in 1933 and from then on held several executive functions within the cavalry of the SS, being an experienced equestrian. During the war he commanded the *8. SS-Kavalerie-Division*, but he became known mainly for being the husband of Eva Braun's sister Gretl whom he married in June 1944. During the last weeks of the war he also was Himmler's liaison officer in the *Führer's* headquarters in Berlin. His successful career came to an end on 29 April 1945 when Hitler had him executed on charges of desertion. When Morgen started investigating Fegelein though, he still was a promising SS officer and one of Himmler's favourites. During his investigation into Von Sauberzweig, Morgen had discovered that large quantities of luxury articles had been sold under suspicious circumstances to the warehouse of the SS by members of the cavalry regiment commanded by Fegelein. Moreover, it transpired that Von Sauberzweig had transferred the management of a confiscated fur company from its Jewish owner to an SS officer from Fegelein's regiment. Those involved claimed that the many international contacts of the firm were being used for espionage purposes, but there was no evidence to support that claim. Self-enrichment by selling fur coats to German customers seemed to be the only goal.[5]

When Morgen launched an investigation into the possible corruption network surrounding Fegelein, he was suddenly taken off the case by Himmler. Fegelein was pardoned and the case was swept under the rug.[6] Undoubtedly Himmler acted in this way because an emerging corruption scandal involving one of his favourite officers would stain the reputation of his SS. The *Reichsführer-SS* wanted to expose the extravagant self-enrichment of his rival Hans Frank and a corruption scandal within his own SS would undermine his position. Since the creation of the General Government there had always been conflicts between the two Nazi leaders. This was in particular due to Himmler's plans with the General Government that did not match those of Frank. Apart from being the leader of the SS, Himmler also was *Reichskommissar für die Festigung Deutschen Volkstums* (commissioner for the settlement of German people). In that capacity, he was responsible for the resettlement of *Volksdeutsche* (ethnic Germans) in the German Empire. These people often had lived outside Germany's borders in eastern Europe for generations, and in Himmler's plans they constituted the new elite in those parts of Poland that had been annexed by Germany. To make room for the settlement of these Germans, Himmler ordered hundreds of thousands of Jews and non-Jewish Poles to be transferred to the General Government, where they were usually left to their own devices.

Frank did not agree to Himmler's using the General Government as a 'racial trash can' and complained to Hermann Göring. Göring agreed with him and stopped all 'evacuations' to the General Government as per 23 March 1940. From then on, transports could only take place with Frank's approval. More conflicts arose between the two until March 1942 when Himmler's hand was strong enough to sidetrack Frank. Himmler enjoyed the support of two powerful colleagues: Martin Bormann, Hitler's unofficial private secretary, and Hans Lammers, chief of the *Reichskanzlei*. On 5 March in the saloon car of Himmler's private train, the trio confronted Frank with a string of charges of corruption and abuse of power, the name of his wife being mentioned frequently as well. They pointed out to him how benevolent they were for not immediately presenting this case to Hitler. Frank was no match for this powerful threesome and met all of Himmler's demands. As to security and 'resettlement' Frank would henceforth play second fiddle to the SS.[7] This paved the way for the mass deportations of Jews to the General Government where they would be murdered in extermination camps from 1942 onwards.

Himmler being able to stop a judicial investigation and to grant pardon to a suspect makes clear to what extent jurisdiction within the SS was subjected to the authority of a single person. Morgen might launch investigations against SS men, but when this displeased Himmler the case could be suspended at any moment. This happened in another investigation by Morgen in the General Government: in his case against Dr Oskar Dirlewanger (1895–1945). After the First World War, this veteran, bearer of the Iron Cross 1st and 2nd class, was active in an ultra-right *Freikorps* (a paramilitary unit consisting of demobilized soldiers) and was involved in quelling communist uprisings in the Saar and Ruhr regions. He joined the NSDAP in 1923 and in 1931 rose to become SS leader in Esslingen.

In 1934 Dirlewanger was sentenced to two years imprisonment for raping a girl under age. After serving his sentence he joined the German *Kondor Legion* in 1937 to fight as a volunteer on the side of the Fascists during the Spanish Civil War. On his return he was incorporated in the SS despite his past as a fornicator. In 1940 he was put in charge of a unit named after him, the *SS-Sonderkommando Dirlewanger*, which initially consisted of convicted poachers. Later on, more hardened criminals such as murderers and rapists were admitted to Dirlewanger's unit. In the General Government, the *SS-Sonderkommando* was initially tasked with supervising thousands of Jewish forced labourers employed in the construction of an anti-tank ditch. Odilo Globocnik, the *SS- und Polizeiführer* in the Lublin district, spoke very highly of Dirlewanger's leadership: 'During the construction of the ditch on the river Bug and the management of the camp for Jews at Dzikow, Dirlewanger commanded his unit in extraordinary fashion.'[8]

As a massive amount of information concerning thievery and crimes of violence against the civilian population in the Lublin district committed by members of Dirlewanger's *SS-Sonderkommando* reached him through the military police, Konrad Morgen decided to launch an investigation. The cases he had taken on previously paled in comparison to what he now discovered. Dirlewanger had his men arrest Jews on suspicion of performing ritual slaughter and then demanded a ransom to set them free. Those who could or would not buy themselves out were executed. In addition, the *Sonderkommando* was guilty of plunder in the Lublin ghetto. The booty was sold back to the original owners. Dirlewanger himself was suspected of having had sexual relations with Jewish girls, which was strictly forbidden by the Nuremberg racial laws.[9]

During the Nuremberg trials, Morgen testified to the atrocities to which Dirlewanger subjected his female prisoners (young Jewish girls). In Morgen's words, Dirlewanger and some of his friends from a *Wehrmacht* supply unit had undressed the women and subjected them to horrific 'scientific experiments'. 'The victims had been injected with strychnine, an extremely toxic substance which causes severe muscle cramps and which is used to poison rats. While Dirlewanger lit a cigarette and looked on, his friends doing the same, they watched these girls die. Immediately afterwards, their bodies were cut into small pieces, mixed with horse meat and made into soap.'[10] Morgen admitted his testimony was based on an assumption, although he had eyewitness accounts at his disposal. Many of Dirlewanger's crimes have been proven, but whether he actually conducted such experiments is unclear. Both during and after the war, strong rumours circulated that the Nazis had produced soap using the body fat of their victims. Actually, there was no question of massive soap production using human fat, although small scale experiments may well have been conducted.[11]

In a confidential letter to his superior Norbert Pohl, dated 2 November 1941, Morgen wrote that the despotism of Dirlewanger in the Lublin district had a negative influence on the economy of the region. His earlier complaints about this to Odilo Globocnik had fallen on deaf ears, he emphasized. Morgen had also approached the *Höhere SS- und Polizeiführer* Friedrich Wilhelm Krüger and asked him for an arrest warrant for Dirlewanger and his entire unit. As it was, Krüger, in his capacity as *SS-Gerichtsherr*, was not authorized to open a case against Dirlewanger and his men. His *SS-Sonderkommando* was the responsibility of Gotlob Berger who, being chief of the *SS-Hauptamt*, was responsible for recruiting men for the *Waffen-SS*. It was Berger who in 1940 had been responsible for Dirlewanger's rehabilitation and had offered him a chance to command his own unit. Berger had no intention of letting his protégé down, but after a telephone conversation with Krüger it was decided to transfer him to Byelorussia.[12] From the autumn of 1942 onwards, Dirlewanger's unit was deployed in the fight against partisans. His violent behaviour, also during the Polish uprising in Warsaw in August and September 1944, was highly praised by his superiors. He rose to *SS-Oberführer* and was awarded the Knight's Cross of the Iron Cross. In June 1945 he was arrested by French authorities and died in prison, probably as a result of torture and poor treatment.

So, Morgen had to cancel his investigation into Dirlewanger as well. Once again he had come up against the dual morality that was being applied by his superiors. It bothered him that whenever he opened a case he could never be sure whether or not he could proceed without being thwarted from above. In a letter of 27 March 1942 to *SS-Obersturmbannführer* Eberhardt Hinderfeld, within the *Hauptamt SS-Gericht* the man responsible for personnel affairs, he asked to be transferred. He wrote: 'The corruption in the General Government is so great and property crimes and offences of a revolting nature so numerous that I am deeply convinced that any judge, in time, must find himself somewhat dulled, and the danger therefore exists that his natural sense of justice will suffer damage. You will therefore understand, *Obersturmbannführer*, that I have the intense desire to live once again in a healthier atmosphere than in the General Government.'[13]

He hoped for a transfer to a judicial post in Norway or in the Balkans but his superiors had something quite different in store for him. He was stripped of his rank of *SS-Obersturmführer*, to which he had been promoted on 20 April 1942, and was downgraded to *SS-Sturmmann* (soldier). He was transferred to a military training camp in Stralsund in northeastern

Germany, and in December 1942 was posted to the 'Germania' regiment of the *Waffen-SS* Division Wiking which was deployed in the southern sector of the Eastern front.[14]

Official documents are not available, but after the war Morgen gave as a reason for his transfer and degradation that Himmler had been angry about the way he had handled a charge against a German police officer in early 1942. The man had been indicted for sexual contact with a Polish woman. Despite Himmler having strictly forbidden intimate relations with Polish women and had pressed for severe penalties, Morgen and his colleagues received numerous similar charges. Morgen considered a severe punishment ridiculous for this transgression and had dismissed the charge.[15] Subsequently Morgen was blamed by his superiors for 'not having the correct political feeling': 'I would not have acted forcibly enough.'[16] It is incorrect to conclude from this that Morgen was a soft-hearted judge. At the close of 1941 he handed down five death sentences over a period of ten days.[17] Himmler though considered Morgen's conduct sabotage of his order and that is the reason why Morgen was relieved of his function and ultimately sent to the front. The *Reichsführer-SS* even threatened him with two to three years imprisonment in a concentration camp, but he refrained from it thanks to protests by Morgen's superiors within the *Hauptamt SS-Gericht*.[18]

According to Morgen, the issue with the police officer had been passed on to Himmler by enemies he had made in the General Government. He suspected *SS-Obergruppenführer* Wilhelm Koppe, supported by Oswald Pohl, to have been the snitch, but what his relation to Koppe had been is unclear.[19] Whatever the case, it is likely that Morgen's investigations had vexed high-ranking SS men as many of them were directly or indirectly involved in the corruption cases that Morgen was unravelling. Discrediting him in the presence of Himmler prevented Morgen from demasking even more high-ranking corrupt SS men. At the front he no longer posed a threat to them. Little is known about the period he served in the Wiking Division at the Eastern front. After the war he recalled the heavy losses suffered by the division and the cruel conduct of soldiers of the Red Army. He called the many foreign volunteers in his regiment – Danes, Belgians, Dutch and Norwegians – 'young idealists defending European culture against the tide of Bolshevism'.[20]

Chapter VII

Rehabilitation

Kranichfeld Castle was the perfect location for a tribunal conducted by the SS. The robust limestone building had just the right atmosphere for the chivalric qualities which Heinrich Himmler wished to imbue into his SS. After it had been ravaged by fire in 1934 it was donated to the SS in 1940. The sober castle was to be reborn as an *NS-Ordensburg*, an elite educational centre for Nazi officers. Prisoners from concentration camp Buchenwald, located some 18 miles to the north, were deployed for the restoration. In September 1944 the castle was the scene of the court case against Karl Otto Koch, the camp commander of Buchenwald. The first step was taken in 1943 when Himmler summoned Konrad Morgen back to Germany where he was fully rehabilitated.

The *Reichsführer-SS* could make good use of Morgen's expertise. 'The *Reichskriminalamt* needed a special expert for the fight against corruption,'[1] so Morgen said. He was reinstated in his rank and posted to the department of economic crimes as a judge. The *Reichskriminalhauptamt* was the central department of the *Kriminalpolizei* (Kripo, criminal investigation) and was based in Berlin. Along with the *Gestapo* and the *Sicherheitsdienst* (SD, security service) it was part of the *Reichssicherheitshauptamt* (RSHA, main office of state security) and dealt with crime fighting, including crimes of violence, offences against morality, homicide, economic crimes and theft. The case for which Morgen's expertise was called upon was a major case of corruption in Buchenwald concentration camp. For Morgen it was the beginning of a string of investigations into corruption and other crimes in German concentration camps. After the war he appeared amazed that it was he, of all people, who had been sent to Buchenwald. 'The *Reichskriminalhauptamt* had obviously not been informed of my past, because if they had I cannot imagine they would entrust a case to me for which I had to go to Buchenwald. Maybe they just wanted to pass off the most unpleasant and difficult cases to the greenhorn so he could prove himself or regret it.'[2]

It is more likely though that Morgen was selected because of the tenacity with which he had conducted investigations into corruption cases against high-ranking SS officials in the General Government. At the time this was not appreciated by Himmler, but things had changed. The fact that Morgen was now allowed to have senior SS officers prosecuted seems to have been part of a general change of policy in the concentration camps. Before the war, concentration camps were mainly destined to imprison political opponents to protect the authority of the National Socialists and for the re-education of social 'undesirables' like criminals, homosexuals and alcoholics. After the outbreak of war, the camps took on a steadily increasing economic function. From the beginning of 1942 onwards, the system of concentration camps was run by the newly established *SS-Wirtschaft und Verwaltungshauptamt* (SS-WVHA, the SS head office for economics and management) headed by Oswald Pohl. 'The emphasis in the concentration camps has now shifted to the economic side,' as Pohl wrote to Himmler on 30 April 1942. 'Mobilization of labourers detained in the camps, initially for the war effort (increased production of armaments) and later for construction work in peace time, becomes increasingly important.'[3]

Prisoners were being employed as forced labourers because a shortage of workers had developed as large numbers of male Germans were drafted into the *Wehrmacht*. These shortages could not be replenished sufficiently by employing German women, prisoners of war and foreign (forced) labourers. As the number of prisoners soared during the war, the concentration camps offered a huge and cheap labour pool. Prisoners were no longer being released after a while, as was still customary before the war. Moreover, they no longer originated only from Germany but from the occupied nations too. Deported Jews were also selected to do forced labour in German factories while their unfit-for-labour countrymen were gassed. Working conditions were harsh and Jewish inmates in particular fell victim to the policy known as *Vernichtung durch Arbeit*, elimination by work. They were forced to work so hard and so long in such deplorable conditions that they died.

As a consequence of the economic deployment of the inmates of concentration camps, the camp management was expected to adapt its policy accordingly. Corruption, random abuse and murder of inmates were no longer undesirable from a disciplinarian point of view, but they undermined the productivity of labour and simultaneously the economic interests of the SS. Himmler ordered therefore productivity of the inmates be increased 'if necessary by additional care and provision of clothing'[4] and the rules for camp employees were enforced more strongly. Arbitrary murder and maltreatment were to be punished more severely. As early as 1935, Himmler had forbidden 'any individual action by SS members against Jews'. Guards in concentration camps had to sign a declaration forbidding them from maltreating inmates.[5] He did not care about the fate of the victims but he thought sadism undermined discipline and hence was to be punished most severely.

In the autumn of 1942 the judicial department of the SS asked Himmler how unauthorized executions of Jews should be dealt with. He answered that in cases with 'purely political motives' the executor need not be punished except when 'enforcement of law and order demands punishment'. When however a person had acted out of 'selfish, sadistic or sexual motives' he should be prosecuted, and if necessary also for murder or manslaughter.[6] It was against this background that Himmler sent Morgen to Buchenwald where camp commander Karl Otto Koch had imposed a reign of terror for years and had made himself a strong suspect for corruption. Someone like him undermined the ideological and economical goals of the SS. That is why Morgen was now given a free hand to thoroughly investigate this high-ranking SS officer. What he encountered was even worse than Himmler could have expected.

Chapter VIII

The Horrors of Buchenwald

Buchenwald was one of the largest concentration camps in Nazi Germany and was opened for inmates from central Germany on 16 July 1937. It was located on a hill in a wooded area near a stone quarry where inmates were put to work. Throughout the existence of the camp, it had housed 230,980 persons from 30 countries.[1] The first camp commander was *SS-Standartenführer* Karl Otto Koch, born 2 August 1897, in Darmstadt. He and his second wife Ilse lived in a luxurious villa in the vicinity of the camp. The fact that he once had been fired as a bank employee on suspicion of embezzlement had never hindered his career in the camp system of the SS. He enrolled in the NSDAP in 1930. Before his appointment as camp commander in Buchenwald, he held the same function in the concentration camps at Columbia-Haus, Esterwegen and Sachsenhausen. He was camp commander of Buchenwald from 1 August 1937 until late November 1941. When Konrad Morgen launched the investigation into his corruption, Koch had already left Buchenwald.

It was not the first time that charges had been brought against the feared camp commander. Koch had been arrested on a charge of corruption as early as the winter of 1941. It was on the order of *SS-Obergruppenführer* Josias Erbprinz zu Waldeck und Pyrmont, the HSSPF in the district where Buchenwald was located. The *SS- und Polizeigerichtshof XXII* in Kassel found ample evidence of corruption and Koch was imprisoned in Gestapo headquarters in Weimar. But Waldeck-Pyrmont's efforts to get Koch sentenced were thwarted by his colleagues. Oswald Pohl and *SS-Brigadeführer* Richard Glücks, who succeeded Theodor Eicke as inspector of the concentration camps, protested to Himmler who sent Waldeck-Pyrmont a telegram ordering Koch's immediate release, and so it happened. Subsequently Pohl sent written congratulations to Koch. In his letter he promised his subordinate he would protect him whenever 'a jobless lawyer would once again stretch out his henchmen's claws to him'.[2] On a visit to Buchenwald, Glücks stated that all accusations regarding

Koch were false. He threatened to punish everyone severely, inmates as well as guards, who brought further charges against Koch. Himmler decided to intervene as well. Henceforth his permission was required for the arrest and prosecution of a camp commander or anyone in the rank of *SS-Standartenführer* or above.[3]

Towards the end of 1941, Koch was transferred to Lublin in Poland to become commander of Majdanek concentration camp. The escape of eighty-four Russian inmates on the night of 14 July 1942 blemished his reputation. Although he had tried to put the blame on two guards, he was ousted anyway. He was transferred to Eger in Hungary where he was reduced to employee of the *SS-Postschutz*, an armed SS unit tasked with guarding the German postal service. Meanwhile the *SS- und Polizeigericht XXII* in Kassel had discovered another case of corruption in which Koch had been involved. The young criminal police investigator Emil Holtschmidt had launched an investigation into *Ortsgruppenleiter* Thilo Bornschein. This local party leader and food merchant was suspected of being involved in various cases of fraud, along with Koch. To prevent the prosecution of Bornschein, Koch had made him a member of the camp's staff. There he would have nothing to fear from Holtschmidt anymore as he, being a police investigator, had no jurisdiction inside the camp. Konrad Morgen though, a judge with an officer's rank in the *Waffen-SS*, did have that authority. In the spring of 1943 he travelled to Weimar, booked a room in Hotel Elephant and was granted entry into the camp. It did not take him long to collect ample evidence against Bornschein to have him sentenced to nine years imprisonment.[4]

Morgen found out that Bornschein was only a small fish compared to camp commander Koch. Together with some cronies, he had enriched himself unscrupulously with the possessions and money of his inmates. He did this for instance by imposing fines on prisoners who were under suspicion of having damaged camp property such as lamps and bedding. The fines disappeared into his own pocket. Sometimes a penalty such as this was imposed on the inmates of an entire block. According to Morgen, inmates would have paid money to Koch and his cronies to avoid physical punishment. In a report about the conditions in Buchenwald, Morgen wrote: 'When [in the small zoo near the camp] a wolf had died and a bear had stumbled into the electric fence, rumours went around that the animals had been killed by inmates with bad intentions. In order to prevent the worst happening, on this occasion alone, thousands of Reichsmarks were supposedly collected.'[5]

Morgen also learned from other witnesses that 'wealthy' *SS-Schutzhaft* inmates, who remained in the camp for a short while only, had offered sizable sums for their release. Koch himself claimed a Jew had offered him a million *Reichsmark* once and had paid it. Every week, hidden jewelry was discovered and embezzled in the camp. Gold rings stolen from inmates were melted down to large chunks. A larger amount of gold originating from the teeth of inmates was collected in the camp hospital and in the crematory. 'There was no registration of gold and jewelry whatsoever,' Morgen stated. 'Against the defendant *SS-Standartenführer* Koch, a serious suspicion exists of him having had golden articles made, especially for his wife.'[6]

Some of the money Koch and his men had appropriated illegally had come from some 10,000 Jews who had been temporarily imprisoned in the camp following *Kristallnacht* in November 1938. Morgen found out that SS officers had 'shamelessly stuffed their pockets and had bled the Jews dry'. He was shocked to learn that nobody had taken any action against it until now, so he took the reins into his own hands. 'I went to the banks in Weimar and had them hand me over all bank statements of the concentration camp and of the personal accounts of *SS-Standartenführer* Koch, although I could not present any order and had no more authority than my uniform. I looked through all papers and I was able to ascertain that Koch had embezzled a sizable amount of money – about 150,000 *Reichsmark* – and had cunningly spread the money over various semiofficial accounts and private accounts as well.'[7]

Morgen discovered in the camp records that quite a number of inmates who might have known about Koch's embezzlements had died. It struck him that a number of prisoners had been admitted to the hospital and the camp prison simultaneously and he concluded that their death certificates had been forged. According to Morgen, 'They were made out so cleverly that any prejudiced reader of the documents would get the impression that the prisoner concerned had actually been treated for and had died of the serious illness which was indicated.'[8] Morgen also discovered that a pair of prisoners who 'had been shot while fleeing' had previously treated the camp commander for syphilis (these inmates worked in the camp as medical orderlies). Probably Koch had them executed out of shame.[9]

Morgen counted some 160 inmates who had been murdered in the camp prison by order of Koch and others, usually by intravenous injection with phenol. The number of inmates who had been killed in the sick bay in a similar way was, according to Morgen, 'impossible to guess'. Another 120 inmates had been 'shot while trying to escape' in the stone quarry of Buchenwald. Morgen concluded that a 'multiple of these executions' were to be considered as 'unlawful killing of prisoners'.[10]

By speaking to witnesses, including inmates and guards, Morgen was informed of the 'barbaric and cruel treatment'[11] inmates had to endure during the time Koch was commander of Buchenwald. In his investigation report he wrote about the 'pedantic haughtiness, the uninhibitedness and the cruel arbitrariness' of Koch which, according to him, 'could be noticed in the most sorrowful way in the treatment of inmates'. 'They [the inmates] sometimes had to stand in the parade ground for hours, sometimes even for days and nights in all kinds of weather,' he wrote in his report. 'It did not matter at all if many of them fell to the ground from exhaustion and were carried back to the prisoners' barracks in large numbers. Being beaten, kicked and chased by dogs was the order of the day. In temperatures way below zero, inmates often had to take off their gloves, causing massive frost bite.'

Morgen claimed that Koch had been warned by 'enough of his men' that such treatment was unjustifiable. Koch dismissed these men as too weak and too soft-hearted. He took pride in being known abroad as the most notorious camp commander.[12] Morgen established that the stone quarry was 'one of the largest torture sites of the concentration camp. Here, inmates were forced to carry heavy stones around in double quick time. They regularly had their hats torn off and subsequently were beaten.' Witnesses told him that one day inmates who had been beaten till they bled were made to stand in front of a piping hot oven so their wounds burned. Camp guards had also witnessed colleagues filling inmates with water and then standing on their stomachs. Inmates tortured in this gruesome way were subsequently shot.[13]

Morgen collected sufficient evidence to have Koch arrested on 24 August 1943. Other members of the staff were also arrested, including Koch's wife Ilse, camp doctor *SS-Hauptsturmführer* Dr Waldemar Hoven and guard *SS-Hauptscharführer* Martin Sommer. It had been camp doctor Hoven who had administered lethal injections to inmates on orders by

Koch. He was regularly assisted in this by Sommer. Many assassinations had taken place in the camp prison, also known as the Bunker. Sommer was in charge of the Bunker and was notorious for his sadism. His nickname was 'the Hangman of Buchenwald'. 'Should there be a Hell for retribution in the hereafter, it could not be worse than the cellblock under Sommer,'[14] an inmate declared. One of Sommer's favourite torturing methods was as follows: the hands of an inmate were bound behind his back and subsequently he was hanged from a tree by his hands for hours on end, resulting in dislocated shoulders and arms. The site where this took place was called the 'singing forest' after the cries of pain from the victims.[15] 'It is undoubtedly true that Sommer carried out his tasks as executioner and torturer with great pride and passion,' Morgen established. 'He took pride in being known as the most cruel and hated person in the camp.'[16]

An important witness of the atrocities in Buchenwald for Morgen was the anti-Fascist Alfred Miller, who had been imprisoned in Buchenwald since 1941. He was employed as a helper in the Bunker and, as he stated himself, 'I had a good idea of what was going on in there'. Initially he distrusted Morgen but he grew convinced of the good intentions of the SS officer when he promised to do everything he could to get him released. The same promise was made by the HSSPF Waldeck-Pyrmont who had previously guaranteed in a written declaration that nothing would happen to Miller and had visited him personally to persuade him to testify. After the war Miller remembered very well the wave of arrests that had taken place in Buchenwald as a result of Morgen's investigation. According to Miller, some former members of the staff had even been recalled from the battle front to stand trial. He stated that prisoners were taken out of the Bunker so its cells could be used for the arrested members of staff. 'That was insufficient so some of them had to be imprisoned in Weimar.'[17] Morgen and Waldeck-Pyrmont kept their promise. Miller was released on 13 March 1944. 'I owe my release to Morgen,' he said after the war. According to him, Morgen's investigation had made a deep impression on the camp guards. He stated: 'SS men shuddered because of Morgen. He was considered the devil.'[18]

Chapter IX

Koch and Accomplices on Trial

As Himmler had given permission for his investigation into corruption and other crimes in Buchenwald, finally things seemed to go smoothly for Konrad Morgen. The handling of the case did not proceed successfully though. Within the concentration camp as well as in court he was thwarted in his attempts to get the suspects sentenced. In the camp one of his key witnesses, *SS-Hauptscharführer* Rudolph Köhler, was found in his cell with severe symptoms of poisoning. He was jailed as he was under suspicion himself. It was rumoured he had committed suicide. He was transferred to the military hospital in Weimar where he died, despite all efforts by the physicians. Morgen immediately assumed this was a case of murder by poisoning. The dead man had incriminating evidence about Dr Waldemar Hoven. Morgen suspected the doctor of having poisoned the man. Conclusive evidence for murder could not be found however and the case was never solved.[1]

In connection with the case in Buchenwald, Morgen also collided with *SS-Sturmbannführer* Dr Werner Paulmann of the *SS- und Polizeigericht* in Kassel. On 2 February 1944 Morgen submitted a written complaint about him to the chief of the *Hauptamt SS-Gericht*, Franz Breithaupt. Morgen reported that the 'previous relationship once called pleasant' between him and Paulmann 'had seriously deteriorated'. The background for the conflict was an arrest warrant, issued by Morgen, for *SS-Hauptscharführer* Gotthold Michael who was charged by Morgen with bribery and handling stolen goods. Paulmann criticized Morgen's investigation who in turn accused his colleague of obstructing his investigation. It probably concerned a professional conflict between the two lawyers. No evidence has been found that there was a conscious obstruction of Morgen's efforts to get camp staff sentenced.

Morgen sent his complaint to Hans Bender as well, the highest SS- and Police judge who was on the staff of the *Reichsführer-SS* (Himmler). In Morgen's view it was a 'serious difference of opinion'. As was customary in those days, Morgen signed his letter with 'Heil Hitler'. On 8 February 1944, Bender sent a letter to the *Hauptamt SS-Gericht* in Munich from Himmler's field headquarters enquiring whether the conflict had been settled. 'I know the *Reichsführer-SS* certainly does not tolerate such differences of opinion and can impose drastic measures,' he wrote in a threatening tone, 'in order to instill the necessary notion of their duties to the causer of this struggle or both if necessary.' The reply to Bender was sent from Munich on 23 February 1944. It was indicated that Paulmann and Morgen were summoned to Breithaupt in Munich to report. In the presence of HSSPF Waldeck-Pyrmont the differences were discussed and settled both professionally and personally. 'A decent cooperation is again guaranteed for the future.'[2]

As late as September 1944, the case against Koch and his accomplices was brought before the *SS- und Polizeigericht zbV* in Weimar which sat temporarily in Kranichfeld Castle. In April, Morgen had submitted his investigation report in which he gave a detailed description of the methods of corruption in Buchenwald. Apart from corruption, Morgen also charged Koch and his cronies with torturing and killing of prisoners on their own initiative. Not Morgen himself but other judges had to pass verdict on the charges he had made. Attending the sessions were Richard Glücks, the inspector of the concentration camps and *SS-Obersturmführer* Kurt Schmidt-Klevenov, chief of the judicial and social department of Oswald Pohl's SS-WVHA. The leadership of the SS-WVHA attempted to prevent their subordinates from being sentenced, just as they did when Koch was arrested in 1941. Schmidt-Klevenov used every trick in the book to play down the charges. In court he claimed that Himmler's order against the unauthorized killing of prisoners should possibly not be taken too literally. Over lunch he declared that Morgen's charges blemished the reputation of the SS and disrupted the smooth functioning of the concentration camps.[3]

For reasons which are unclear, the case was postponed until 19 December 1944. Meanwhile Morgen had been transferred to Krakow and was involved in the case as a witness only. The ultimate verdict was a disappointment for him: Karl and Ilse Koch were only indicted by the court for corruption and not, as Morgen had wished, for unauthorized killing of prisoners. Ilse was acquitted due to lack of evidence while her husband was pronounced guilty and sentenced to death. On 5 April 1945, barely a week before the liberation of the camp by the Americans, he was executed by an SS firing squad.[4]

Compared to their former camp commander, Dr Waldemar Hoven and Martin Sommer were punished less severely by the SS. Their cases were heard apart from that of Koch. Dr Hoven was imprisoned in Buchenwald until the case against him was dropped in March 1945 and he resumed his work as a camp doctor. He was arrested by the Americans after the war, and during the Doctors' Trial in Nuremberg he was pronounced guilty of war crimes, crimes against humanity and membership of a criminal organization – the SS. On 20 August 1947 the court sentenced him to death. The sentence was carried out on 2 June 1948 in Landsberg.[5] Sommer was imprisoned by the SS as well until March 1945 when he was placed in a penal unit of the *Waffen-SS* and sent to the front where he lost an arm and a leg. After the war it was decided initially not to prosecute him for reasons of health, but in 1958 he was subpoenaed nonetheless by the West-German authorities. On 3 July 1958 he was sentenced to life imprisonment – the most severe penalty in West-Germany – for having murdered at least twenty-five inmates by intravenous injections with evipan, phenol and air. He was released ahead of time in 1971 and passed away in a residential home for the elderly near Nuremberg on 7 June 1988.[6]

The case against Koch and his accomplices also took Morgen to Majdanek concentration camp, bordering on Lublin in western Poland, where Koch had been camp commander between September 1941 until August 1942. In this camp, established in 1941, which also served as an extermination camp, a total of some 500,000 inmates from 28 countries had been imprisoned. About 360,000 of them perished in the camp: 60 per cent of illnesses, torture, starvation and exhaustion, 40 per cent murdered in the gas chambers or by firing squad.[7] Morgen established that Koch and his members of staff had continued their corruption activities, 'illegal murders' and atrocities. He noted for instance that in the camp crematory, inmates were beaten to death with steel bars and that their corpses were cut to pieces.[8] During his investigation in Majdanek he was thwarted once again: all potential Jewish witnesses had reportedly been put to death before they could present evidence against the camp management.[9] Nonetheless, ample incriminating evidence was presented to have former staff member *SS-Obersturmführer* Hermann Hackmann arrested. Hackmann was serving in the *Waffen-SS* at the time but he had been employed in both Buchenwald and Majdanek as a staff member of Koch. On 29 June 1944 the *SS- und Polizeigericht* in Kassel pronounced him guilty of embezzlement and sentenced him to death. Things did not go that far as he was released from the prison camp in Dachau before the end of the war and placed in a penal unit.[10]

Chapter X

Florstedt's Mysterious Fate

Another colleague of Karl Otto Koch who had been arrested in connection with the investigation into corruption was Hermann Florstedt. Born on 18 February 1895, this businessman had joined the NSDAP and the SS in 1931. At the outbreak of war he was admitted to the ranks of the *Waffen-SS*, in charge of the guard unit in Buchenwald. From 1 July 1940 onwards he was employed as *Schutzhaftlagerführer* in Sachsenhausen and Buchenwald. On 25 November 1942 he succeeded Max Kögel as commander of Majdanek. As late as 20 April 1943 he was promoted to *SS-Sturmbannführer*. The nomination for his promotion read: 'With his ambitious, diligent and energetic nature he has shaped this camp [Majdanek] into an impeccable condition. Florstedt has proved to be extremely useful also as camp commander in a difficult camp.'

This view was shared by Odilo Globocnik, the *SS-und Polizeiführer* in the Lublin district, who wrote in 1943 it was due to Florstedt that 'the unacceptable situations that prevailed in the camp [Majdanek] at the time, had been solved'. Despite Florstedt being praised by his superiors for having put a stop to the chaos that had been prevalent in Majdanek when Koch was still in charge, he did not escape from Morgen's charges. On 23 October 1943 it was reported to the *SS-Personalhauptamt* that Florstedt 'had been arrested by order of Himmler on charges of embezzlement and other serious crimes, that he had been taken to Buchenwald by judge Morgen for interrogation'. However, in Florstedt's personnel file of the SS, nothing can be found about what happened to him after that.[1]

Florstedt's fate is still unclear today. Many historians assume he was executed by the SS in Buchenwald in 1945, like Koch. Peter Lindner, the author of Florstedt's biography, does not believe so: he is convinced that 'Florstedt survived under an alias and possibly passed away in peace'.[2] His assumption is not unfounded. It is based on a claim by Florstedt's wife after the war that her husband worked for the *Kriminalpolizei* in a major city in West Germany under a false name. Hermann Florstedt's sister-in-law reportedly also claimed she had given him clothing in April 1945 and that he subsequently had gone into hiding. Charlotte Florstedt probably committed suicide in 1959 and therefore Lindner could not ask her for more information for his book, published in 1997. West-German authorities also have taken into account that Florstedt might possibly have survived. In January 1962 the public prosecutor of the *Oberlandesgericht* in Cologne launched an investigation into him on suspicion of murders he had committed while being employed in Sachsenhausen concentration camp. In February 1962 the *Zentralstelle der Landesjustizverwaltung* in Ludwigsburg, charged with the prosecution of National Socialist crimes, reported: 'According to the testimony of various witnesses before the end of the war, Florstedt was executed in concentration camp Buchenwald.'[3] As conclusive evidence as to his execution or his demise has never been found anywhere, the case is not yet closed.

In the same year the West-German authorities launched their investigation into Florstedt, a private person did likewise. His name was Joseph Jenniges, a former member of the Catholic *Zentrumpartei* and Christian labour union man who had been imprisoned in Buchenwald from 1940 until his liberation by the Americans. He was convinced Florstedt had survived the war. He claimed he had seen him in the camp as late as April 1945 where the SS officer could move around at will. Afterwards the SS man would have escaped from the camp to evade arrest by the Americans. Before his departure he had been responsible for the death of a number of young women, so Jenniges claims. They had been hanged in the crematory and burned. Their bodies were allegedly still burning when the Americans entered the camp. Jenniges had learned of the rumour that after the war Florstedt had been employed by the *Kriminalpolizei* in Mainz, as had been reported in an article in the *Thüringer Tageblatt*. Therefore he asked confirmation in writing from the president of the police in Mainz. The latter replied on 12 December 1962 that someone bearing the name Florstedt had never been employed by the police in Mainz or its surroundings. The public prosecutor of the *Oberlandesgericht* in Cologne adopted this point of view.

Numerous persons who had dealt with Florstedt, including Konrad Morgen, claimed he had been executed during the war. On 9 April 1963 Morgen wrote a letter to the public prosecutor in Cologne, saying Florstedt had been sentenced and executed by the SS. According to Dr Günther Reinecke, chief of the *Oberste SS- und Polizeigericht*, Florstedt had been sentenced and executed for the crimes he had committed in Majdanek as early as 1943. The 'Hangman of Buchenwald', Martin Sommer, also stated on 15 July 1963 that Florstedt had been executed before the end of the war. He argued that Florstedt, along with Koch, had been transferred to Buchenwald on 3 April 1945, where both had been executed by order of Dr Werner Paulmann. Like Morgen, Sommer had not been present at the execution; he had learned of it on 6 April 1945 from the camp doctors Dr Erwin Ding-Schuler and Dr Waldemar Hoven. The first committed suicide in 1945, the latter was executed in 1948, so neither could be asked for more information. Some former inmates came up with other explanations, one of them claiming that Florstedt had been hanged in public by the Russians in Weimar.[4] This cannot be dismissed entirely. Although Buchenwald had been liberated by the Americans, shortly afterwards the camp was handed over to the Russians and put to use as a 'special camp' of the NKVD, the Russian secret service.

As no conclusive evidence has been found that Florstedt survived the war, the West-German judicial authorities closed the case against him on 15 October 1963. In the archives of the Stasi, the East German secret service, there is also an entry that Florstedt died: he allegedly was killed when the inmates of the camp revolted shortly before the liberation of the camp. Peter Lindner however correctly claims there is no dependable evidence as to Florstedt's execution or demise. The sources on which he bases his conviction that the former camp commander survived the war are serious enough to consider the possibility that he is right. Therefore Florstedt cannot be mentioned with complete certainty as one of the camp commanders who was sentenced and executed as a result of Konrad Morgen's investigations.

Chapter XI

The Blood Judge

The Buchenwald case was the beginning of a series of criminal investigations into corruption and other crimes in German concentration camps during 1943 and 1944. By order of Himmler, Morgen was tasked with 'launching investigations into all … punishable acts in concentration camps', as he described it himself, and 'all political and judicial authorities were ordered to hand over those kinds of cases to me.'[1] Special investigative committees of SS lawyers, coordinated by Konrad Morgen, set off to concentration camps to gather evidence to be submitted to the responsible SS and Police courts. Morgen had some fifty people at his disposal, they were answerable to the *SS- und Polizeigericht zur besonderer Verwendung* (SS and police court for special purposes) which initially was part of the *SS- und Polizeigericht* in Kassel and later on part of the *Hauptamt SS-Gericht*.[2] Morgen, who initially remained in the employment of the court in Kassel, had jurisdiction in all SS districts, both within and outside German borders, and had permission to enter each and every camp with or without permission from the management. 'Only very few people had this permission,' he stated at the Nuremberg trial. 'Before beginning an investigation I examined the concentration camp in question in all its details very closely, inspecting those arrangements which seemed particularly important to me. I visited them repeatedly and without notice.' Each investigation took much time. 'I was working mostly in Buchenwald itself for eight months and have lived there. I was in Dachau for one or two months.' Other camps where he conducted an investigation included Auschwitz, Sachsenhausen, Vught, Krakau, Płaszów and Warsaw.[3]

According to Morgen, his work earned him the nickname 'the blood judge' within the SS.[4] He claimed to have taken on 800 cases (often involving numerous suspects) of which 200 resulted in sentencing by the court. Far from all of these cases were against SS officers: in the end only a few camp commanders were prosecuted, of whom, according to

Morgen, only two were executed (Koch and Florstedt). A death sentence would also have been pronounced against other officers and non-commissioned officers but he mentioned no names.[5] German historian Heinz Höhne discovered the names of various camp commanders against whom Morgen had launched an investigation. Apart from Koch and Florstedt, they were Amon Göth, Adam Grünewald, Karl Künstler, Alex Piorkowski and Hans Loritz.[6] All five were relieved as camp commander by the SS during the war. The impression has emerged that all these men were taken to court as a result of Morgen's investigation only to be fired afterwards, but as far as Künstler, Piorkowski and Loritz are concerned, the truth lies elsewhere. Morgen launched his investigation only after they had been fired by Oswald Pohl, who had replaced about one third of his camp commanders, mostly because of incompetence.[7] Ultimately none of those three seem to have been sentenced as a result of Morgen's charges.

As early as August 1942, *SS-Obersturmbannführer* Karl Künstler had been relieved of his post as camp commander of Flossenbürg concentration camp for abuse of alcohol.[8] Morgen had nothing to do with this discharge as he had started his investigations in the concentration camps in 1943. Künstler had been commander in Flossenbürg since 1939, and in 1935 he had been employed in the *Frühe Konzentrationslager* Columbia Haus in Berlin-Tempelhof.[9] Himmler was also informed of Künstler's alcohol addiction. Himmler's attitude towards excessive use of alcohol was twofold: at the front he thought use of alcohol 'acceptable within limits and sometimes necessary for reasons of health'. When, however, as a result of abuse of alcohol, missteps were committed, his judgment was merciless: 'Either you show you can handle alcohol and adapt or your pistol will be sent back to you and you end your life.' Actually he was usually more lenient and merely banned them from drinking alcohol. In 1941 he established a detox centre in concentration camp Buchenwald for SS men with alcohol problems.[10] The SS leader was also aware of Künstler's drinking problem. 'When the [*Reichsführer-SS*] hears about [Künstler's] orgies and drinking excesses …, he'll be locked up for years,' as Himmler's adjutant reported to Oswald Pohl.[11] It was not to be, however: Künstler served in the *7. SS-Divison Prinz Eugen* from 1942 to 1945. He was killed in action in April 1945.[12]

According to Heinz Höhne, *SS-Sturmbannführer* Alex Piorkowski was indicted by Morgen 'for murder but not sentenced'.[13] Piorkowski had been *Schutzhaftlagerführer* in Lichtenburg concentration camp (closed in 1939) since February 1938. From September 1938 he had held the same rank in Dachau until he was promoted to camp commander in 1940. In the summer of 1942 he was replaced and relieved of active duty, probably in connection with charges of corruption. Morgen cannot have been involved in Piorkowski's discharge as camp commander as he was still at the front himself at the time. Further details of an SS case against Piorkowski are unknown. After the war the former camp commander was indicted by the Americans during a tribunal in the former Dachau concentration camp, once his workplace, where they had established a prison camp for Nazi war criminals. Along with a few other former staff members of Dachau, Piorkowski was indicted, among other things, for having selected disabled inmates to be gassed, the mass execution of Soviet PoWs and involvement in medical experiments on human guinea pigs. Piorkowski received a death sentence which was carried out in Landsberg on 22 October 1948.[14]

Heinz Höhne claimed *SS-Oberführer* Hans Loritz, commander of Oranienburg concentration camp, had been charged by Morgen 'with serious suspicion of manslaughter'.[15] Oranienburg was the name, frequently used, of Sachsenhausen concentration camp, established in 1936 and located in Oranienburg near Berlin. Loritz was camp commander from April 1940 onwards.[16] He was relieved of his post in August 1942 because of corruption: he had employed forced labourers in the construction of a yacht for himself. As early as 1939 he had been discharged as camp commander in Dachau, officially because of his cruel treatment of inmates.[17] At the time, he also allegedly deployed inmates to build his luxurious villa Waldheim in St. Gilgen on Lake Wolfgang in Austria.[18] Morgen cannot have been involved in Loritz's discharge in 1939 and 1942. It must be assumed that the SS judge would have launched an investigation into him in 1943 or 1944. There are indications that his investigative committee had been frustrated in Sachsenhausen, as in Buchenwald. The members of his committee would have been expelled from Sachsenhausen by physical violence.[19] Also, an inmate acting as an informer for Morgen was saved from the gallows at the last minute. The camp management had intended to kill him to dissuade inmates from cooperating with Morgen.[20] Morgen was not able to achieve much in the case against Loritz: after his transfer he was active in Norway to supervise forced labourers and camps for PoWs until the end of the war. He committed suicide in a prison camp in Neumünster on 31 January 1946.[21]

Chapter XII

The Bunker Tragedy in Vught

After the war, Konrad Morgen claimed he had launched an investigation into *SS-Sturmbannführer* Adam Grünewald, commander of Camp Vught in the occupied Netherlands as well. Although Morgen's actual role in the prosecution of Grünewald by the SS is unclear and probably minor, the case against this camp commander is characteristic for the jurisdiction within the SS and shows clear similarities with the cases in which Morgen had far more influence. That is why this case is dealt with here.

Adam Grünewald, son of a carpenter, was born on 20 October 1902 in Frickenhausen near Würzburg, and made a turbulent career in the SS. After the First World War he served from 1919 until 1931 in the *Reichswehr* as a foot soldier and rose to the rank of *Feldwebel* – sergeant. After ending his active service in the army, he was active in a *Freikorps* and became a member of the NSDAP and the SA on 1 May 1931. His rank was *SA-Obersturmbannführer*. On 12 September 1934 he transferred to the SS. After his transfer he became *SS-Sturmhauptführer*, which was later that year renamed *SS-Hauptsturmführer*. He served in the *Politische Bereitschaft* – the forerunner of the *Waffen-SS* – until 10 November 1934 when he was transferred to Lichtenburg concentration camp near Wittenberg in east Germany. He was in charge of a company of guards. He was totally unsuited for this rank as on 13 July 1935 Theodor Eicke, the inspector of the concentration camps, asked the *SS-Personalamt* for his transfer. In his opinion Grünewald was unable to 'lead his company correctly and raise it to military level. ... although having been a soldier in the *Reichswehr* ... he lacks the ability to be deployed in the garrison force of the SS as an officer.' If a suitable position could not be found for him, a civil position would have to be found. It took until 10 July 1937 before another position was found.

Despite his unsuitability having been established by Theodor Eicke, Grünewald was appointed leader of a company once again, this time in the *SS-Totenkopfverband* Thüringen, an armed unit employed for guarding Buchenwald, among other things. Here he stood out for his incompetence again. He was marked unsuitable to serve as an officer at the front and for a position in a concentration camp: 'He lacks the necessary harshness for dealing with enemies of the state.' He was then registered for training as *SS-Sturmbannführer* in the *Allgemeine-SS*, the civil branch of the SS. Grünewald was far from being a star of the training course he took in Dachau from 26 February 1938 onwards, especially in the intellectual field. In his evaluation of 8 April it was noted that although he might have been dependable and in possession of a good will and a comradely attitude, because of his 'severely limited mental abilities … a lengthier education and training at a school for officers will not achieve the desired result'. He was found suitable to train smaller units but was not eligible for promotion to *SS-Sturmbannführer*. Subsequently he found employment for a while in the Austrian *Allgemeine-SS* until he was transferred to Dachau concentration camp in May 1938 where he had been appointed by Richard Glücks, Eicke's successor, to second *Schutzhaftlagerführer*. Once again it was established that this job did not suit him. His direct superior in Dachau stated that Grünewald showed 'little interest' in his work. 'Grünewald will never become an independent *Schutzhaftlagerführer* while he takes no interest in anything at all and shows no sense of responsibility.' As no other position could be found for him however, he remained in this function for the time being.

The war offered new opportunities for Grünewald's career. In November 1939 the SS man, initially trained as a baker, was appointed leader of the bakers' company of the *SS-Totenkopfdivision*. In this capacity he took part in the campaign in the west and ultimately ended up on the eastern front. Finally, he earned some praise: on 26 July 1940, he was awarded the Iron Cross 2nd class, and on 2 August 1941 his commander recommended him for promotion to *SS-Sturmbannführer*: 'Due to the magnificent leadership of the company – by Grünewald – this unit executed the orders allotted to it always and in any situation in a most able manner. In addition, *SS-Hauptsturmführer* Grünewald succeeded in raising the company to most respectable levels of militarism, world-view and sportsmanship.'

The promotion was approved, effective from 1 September. Although it seemed he had finally found his feet, on 20 November 1942 he was transferred to *Amtsgruppe D* of the SS-WVHA, responsible for the concentration camps. Following his initial employment as *Schutzhaftlagerführer* in Sachsenhausen, he was appointed commander of Herzogenbusch concentration camp, better known as Camp Vught.[1] He replaced former camp commander *SS-Hauptsturmführer* Karl Walter Chmielewski who had been discharged in October 1943 on suspicion of embezzlement.[2] It would not take long though before Grünewald was also fired as camp commander, and he had to answer for a serious incident, the so-called bunker tragedy which had occurred in his camp.

Camp Vught, established in 1942, was the only camp in the occupied Netherlands modelled after the concentration camps in Germany. The first inmates arrived in January 1943 and in consequence of the deplorable conditions most perished in the first few months. Between January 1943 and September 1944 the camp housed over 31,000 inmates for a shorter or longer period. Amongst the inmates were some 12,000 Jews who were deported from the camp to the extermination camps in Poland, usually through Westerbork transit camp. A total of 421 inmates died in the camp from hunger, disease and maltreatment; 329 inmates were executed on the execution site outside the camp. Compared to the concentration camps in Germany and Poland, the mortality rate was low. The German administration in the Netherlands, headed by *Reichskommissar* Arthur Seyss-Inquart, assisted by *Höhere SS- und Polizeiführer* Hanns Albin Rauter, considered Camp Vught a model camp. The relatively less harsh regime and the avoidance of excesses were to prevent the Dutch from objecting to the presence of the camp.[3]

'The political relations in the Netherlands require ... an exceptionally delicate attitude as occurrences in the camp will not remain hidden from the outside world,' so the court established that dealt with the case against Grünewald. Among others, the Dutch camp guards provided society with information about events within the camp. This information 'could to a great extent be used by enemy propaganda in an extraordinary way, considerably disrupting the goals of the *Reichskommissar* in the Netherlands.'[4] Before his appointment as camp commander, Grünewald had been informed about the political situation in the Netherlands and the consequences for him, but on the night of 15/16 January 1944, things went horribly wrong nonetheless.

Shortly before the bunker tragedy, a quarrel had erupted in the women's department of the camp. One of the female inmates in barrack 23 had been charged with treason by the other women and they had cut her hair as punishment. Next day, the prime culprit was locked up by the camp management in the prison of the camp, the Bunker. She refused to reveal the names of the other women who had been involved in the quarrel. The women in barrack 23 decided to act in sympathy and declared themselves guilty, expecting to mitigate the punishment of their co-prisoner. That turned out be a fatal mistake as Grünewald considered the act of solidarity on the part of the women as mutiny and decided to intervene extremely harshly. Encouraged by *SS-Obersturmführer* Hermann Wicklein, he had all the women rounded up on 15 January and locked up in two cells in the Bunker. Seventy-four women were crammed into cell 115 while the other seventeen were locked up in nearby cell 117. Usually cell 115 was meant for two to three prisoners. With an area of less than 98 square feet, the women were forced to stand packed close to each other and were unable to lie down. There was hardly any ventilation.[5] Tineke Wibaut survived the tragedy. She remembered panic breaking out 'in full force' when the light in the cell went out. 'It was an eerie swelling sound, diminishing a little from time to time and then swelling again. It was produced by praying, screaming and yelling women. Some tried to shout and warn the other women to stay calm and not to waste oxygen. Sometimes it helped, albeit only for a short time, and then it started again. It did not stop throughout the night, just a little less loud. The heat became suffocating.'[6]

Next day, towards 07:00 hours, the door to cell 115 was opened. Some women were able to leave the cell on their own, others remained on the floor, motionless. The bodies were dragged from the cell. The camp doctor, who had rushed in, could save only twenty unconscious victims, but ten others had not survived the night. On 21 January the camp doctor performed an autopsy on the corpses, assisted by two *Luftwaffe* physicians. They established that during the long period of standing upright, blood had drained from the upper parts of the women's bodies resulting in unconsciousness. In addition, they stated that as a result of the panic that had erupted, an increased consumption of oxygen had occurred which could not be replenished due to the poor ventilation.[7] Grünewald had attempted to put the blame on the women and sweep the issue under the rug by falsifying the death certificates. Two of his staff members reported to the SD in The Hague although he had forbidden them to talk about the death of the women. On 24 January Grünewald was summoned by Rauter to report.[8] The report, made up by the camp commander and his colleagues, leaked like a sieve: the precise number of deaths was suppressed, as was the fact that Grünewald had forbidden the windows of the cell to be opened. The report also stated that the cells were 'comparatively large and spacious'.[9] Rauter did not allow himself to be fooled and reportedly had been furious about Grünewald's behaviour. A close associate of the HSSPF declared: 'He [Rauter] was furious about so much inhumanity and called Grünewald a monster that should be locked up.'[10]

Rauter informed Himmler's staff about the event. The case was apparently taken seriously enough to cause the RFSS to pay a personal visit to the camp on 3 February. The fear the incident would become known among the Dutch population became a reality on 15 February when the underground paper *Vrij Nederland* was the first to report it. Other illegal papers would also write about it later on. On 21 February, Grünewald was discharged as camp commander and replaced by *SS-Sturmbannführer* Hans Hüttig. Konrad Morgen set off for Vught to launch an investigation.[11] Little is known about the duration of his investigation and his findings. During the trial in Nuremberg he only stated he had visited the camp. He also claimed Oswald Pohl had said to him: 'What do the lives of ten women matter in view of the thousands of German women dying every night in the air raids?'[12] Despite Pohl's attempts to block it, the trial against Grünewald and his fellow suspect Hermann Wicklein was opened on 6 March 1944. The case was taken on by the *SS- und Polizeigericht X* in The Hague but took place in Velp, Gelderland, near Arnhem, to where the court had been transferred in February 1944. The court was chaired by SS judge *SS-Sturmbannführer* Look, assisted by two lay judges.[13] The court's verdict was characteristic for the jurisdiction within the SS.

After pointing to the special political situation in the Netherlands, the court established meticulously and truthfully what had occurred during that night. The exact measurements of the cell, the number of women locked up, the number of deaths as well as the cause of death, as established by the camp physician, all of it was duly enumerated in the court's proceedings. It was noted that Grünewald had expressly forbidden the cell windows to be opened and that he had warned the women he would have them doused with a firehose if they didn't keep quiet. In view of the economic importance of the concentration camp it was noted that during the next few days 'many of the surviving women ... were unable to be deployed in the allocation of labour in industry, causing a considerable drop in productivity of the hand dynamo shop in the factory of Philips...'. Grünewald's attempts to sweep the case under the rug were mentioned as well, although, according to the court, it had been Wicklein who had asked the camp doctor 'whether it was possible to have some of the women succumb to another cause of death afterwards in order to avoid a scandal'.

Before the court reached a verdict, the limits of 'disciplinary authority' of camp commanders were determined. In case the situation called for it, 'camp commanders were authorized to enforce penalties that might be considerably detrimental to physical well-being'. Such physical penalties were legal and 'can never be penalized as abuse'. That was not the case however when 'enforcing disciplinary measures will lead to damage to a person's health which exceeds the legal limit. The incarceration of a multitude of inmates in a cell, withholding the opportunity to sit and sleep, may in and of itself be considered a necessary measure under the circumstances. ... If however the penalized inmate is physically unable to stand the penalty without considerable damage to his health ... then this exceeds the limits of the acceptable.'

In the opinion of the court, Grünewald had exceeded that limit as he should have known that the air supply in the cells, usually meant for a few people, was insufficient for more than twenty persons. He knew that the ventilation system hardly functioned, or not at all, and yet he had forbidden the opening of the windows. Moreover, he also could have ascertained that numerous women 'because of their age and physical condition' were unable to stand the penalty. Hence the court ruled Grünewald had exceeded the permitted extent of violence, so his conduct was rated as abuse.

The court opted for leniency as it was convinced that Grünewald had not wanted 'the death of the women'. Reference was made to Grünewald's years of service in the *Reichswehr* and his military deployment in the SS where he 'had stood his ground'. The court was fully convinced that Grünewald's action 'did not stem in the least from dishonorable motives'. He was found guilty of involuntary manslaughter, but he was sentenced to only 3.5 years in prison. Although Wicklein was considered the initiator of the penalty and, according to the court, 'morally speaking the guiltiest', he got away with six months in prison as not he but Grünewald, being his superior, bore the judicial responsibility. Both men were not imprisoned for long, as Himmler ordered their release as early as March. For reasons unclear, Himmler ordered Wicklein's case to be reopened, but it never came to be. Until the end of the war he was employed as adjutant in Flossenbürg concentration camp. He survived the war and lived in Oberhausen after 1945.[14] Grünewald was allowed to spend eight days with his family and subsequently took a short training course in Breslau. He then served from June onwards in the *3. SS-Panzerdivision Totenkopf* in the lowest rank of *SS-Mann*. In October 1944 he was promoted to *SS-Obersturmführer*, two ranks below the one he held as camp commander. It is assumed he was killed at the front in Hungary on 22 January 1945.[15]

Chapter XIII

Aktion Reinhard and Erntefest

In the autumn of 1943 Konrad Morgen found out for the first time, according to himself, about the mass murder of the Jews. He found two traces: one led him to Lublin and the other to Auschwitz. Apart from his investigation in Majdanek concentration camp in connection with the corruption network around Koch, Morgen also occupied himself that autumn with a case in a Jewish labour camp, not named by him, in Lublin. During the Nuremberg Trial, Morgen testified he had been informed of the case in a report of the local commander of the *Sicherheitspolizei*. In it mention was made of a Jewish wedding with 1,100 guests. Allegedly there had been talk of 'gluttonous consumption of food and alcoholic drinks'. Morgen shared that view, foreseeing 'a big case of criminal corruption' and left for Lublin. Local police only disclosed the wedding had taken place in a camp of the *Deutsche Ausrüstungswerke*. This SS enterprise, producing army uniforms among other things, managed various labour camps in and around Lublin where Jews were forced to work. In charge of these camps was Christian Wirth, also the inspector of the extermination camps of Belzec, Sobibor and Treblinka in eastern Poland. These camps had been established in late 1941 and in 1942 to carry out *Aktion Reinhard*, the extermination of the Jews in the General Government.

Being a witness at the Nuremberg Trial, Morgen testified he had asked Wirth 'whether this report [about this Jewish marriage] was true or what it meant'. 'To my great astonishment, Wirth admitted this wedding had taken place in the presence of his subordinates. I asked him why he permitted members of his command to do such things and Wirth then revealed to me that on the Führer's orders he had to carry out the extermination of Jews.' The marriage was intended to mislead the Jews as 'one has to fight the Jews with their own weapons, that is to say one has to cheat them', so Wirth explained. It was his strategy to win the Jews who worked for him over to his side with special privileges to make them believe they would stay alive and not lay down their work. Misleading Jews was daily practice also in the three extermination camps of *Aktion Reinhard*. 'The people arriving there had the impression of entering a city or a township,' Morgen learned from Wirth. 'The train drove into a dummy railroad station. After the escorts and the train personnel had left the area, the cars were opened and the Jews got out.' Then they were surrounded by Jewish labourers and Wirth or one of his representatives delivered a reassuring speech in which, according to Morgen, something like the following was said every time: 'Jews, you were brought here to be resettled, but before we organize this future Jewish State, you must of course learn how to work... . You must learn a new trade. You will be taught that here. Our routine here is, first, everyone must take off his clothes so that your clothing can be disinfected, and you can have a bath so that no epidemics will be brought into the camp.'

Wirth told Morgen that the Jews were not going to take a shower at all but that once men and women were separated they went to their deaths. They were to hand in their clothing and everyone was given a receipt so that they believed they would get their belongings back. In the end they entered a large room that looked like a shower room. Once everyone was inside, the doors were closed and an engine was started which blew its exhaust gases with the toxic carbon monoxide into the room. As soon as everyone was dead, the room was ventilated. When the air was breathable again, Jewish labourers removed the bodies. Gold teeth were extracted and the openings of the bodies were checked for valuables. Finally, the corpses were disposed of. During the first few months they were buried in mass graves, but later on, to entirely eradicate the traces of the mass extermination, they were burned in large open air pits (in Belzec and Sobibor from the autumn of 1942 onwards and in Treblinka starting in March 1943). Initially Morgen could not believe Wirth's explanation until he visited a camp in Lublin, where the possessions of the murdered Jews were being collected. 'From the quantity – there were an enormous number of watches piled up – I had to realize that something frightful was going on here,' he declared. 'I was shown the valuables. I can say that I never saw so much money at one time, especially foreign money – all kinds of coins, from all over the world. In addition, there were a gold-smelting furnace and really prodigious bars of gold.'[1]

Numerous witnesses confirmed that the guards in the camps of *Aktion Reinhard* enriched themselves with the valuables which had been taken from their victims. One of them was Stanislaw Szmajzner, who was deployed in Sobibor at the age of 14 as a goldsmith. SS men, including camp commander Franz Stangl, brought him gold that should have been transferred to the *Reichsbank* and ordered him to make something personal for them. Often it included 'gold teeth covered in blood like they had been wrenched from the people's jaws'.[2] He had to turn the gold into jewelry. 'I knew this work was our only salvation,' Szmajzner declared after the war. 'I worked day and night. It was a question of making yourself indispensable. And they all wanted golden trinkets. Oh yes, I am sure I have made things for Stangl. I can't remember what anymore, but they all ordered things like jewelry or monograms for the handbags of their wives and children.'[3]

From the testimony of Abraham Kszepicki, it transpires that similar events also occurred in Treblinka. In the eighteen days he was imprisoned here (later on he escaped from the camp) he witnessed how some Germans took pleasure in collecting 'curiosities'. They were keen on gold watches or 'they would pick out a particularly unusual ring or some other item of women's jewellery, no doubt as a gift to their sweethearts in the Fatherland.' According to Kszepicki, both German as well as Ukrainian guards appropriated much money. 'I think that they all became millionaires in Treblinka.'[4]

For Konrad Morgen it could have been a case larger than that of Buchenwald, but there are no indications that he had visited the extermination camps in the Lublin area. In October 1943, the autumn of the year of Morgen's visit to Wirth, *Aktion Reinhard* was terminated. Most Jews from the General Government had been exterminated and the capacity of Auschwitz was largely sufficient for the gassing of the remaining Jews from other parts of Europe. Belzec, Sobibor and Treblinka were closed down in the spring of 1943, in October 1943 and in July 1943 respectively. The traces of the mass murder had been erased: the corpses had been exhumed and cremated in large open-air pits, barracks were torn down and fir trees planted on the former camp grounds. Nothing remained to show that in these three locations an estimated 1.7 million Jews and an unknown number of Romani people had been murdered. Despite the guards having appropriated numerous valuables, enough was left over for the *Reich*. Odilo Globocnik, the leader of the operation, reported to Himmler on 5 January 1944 that the operation had yielded 178,754,960.59 *Reichsmark* in money, gold and other valuables that had been taken from the victims. 6,415 pounds of gold bars and 41,300 pounds of silver bars had been collected in addition to 16,000 diamonds.[5]

In the autumn of that year, Christian Wirth left for the Adriatic coast where his boss, Odilo Globocnik, had been appointed *Höhere SS- und Polizeiführer*. Along with other former co-workers of *Aktion Reinhard* he occupied himself with not only fighting partisans but with hunting down Jews and political opponents as well. In November 1943 he returned to the Lublin district for a while to contribute to *Aktion Erntefest* (harvest festival).[6] This operation was meant to exterminate all Jews still remaining in the Lublin district. It was aimed at 42,000 to 45,000 prisoners in Majdanek concentration camp and in the Trawniki and Poniatowa labour camps, where they were kept alive to do forced labour. During a conference on 19 October 1943, called by Governor Hans Frank, these camps were considered 'a great danger'. It was feared that Jewish inmates would escape or revolt, as happened in Sobibor on 14 October. In the course of that uprising, twelve SS men and two Ukrainian guards had been killed; some 200 inmates had managed to escape and reach the nearby forest – about fifty of them survived the war.[7] To avoid a repetition, Himmler had ordered the extermination of all living Jews in Poland. As the extermination camps in the Lublin district were no longer operational, the victims were executed on 3 and 4 November on the spot by firing squads. Only some 2,000 Jews survived the mass executions and remained in the *Luftwaffe* labour camps in the Lublin district thereafter.[8]

There are indications that Morgen was a witness to *Aktion Erntefest*. Before the Nuremberg trial, Ernst Kaltenbrunner, who succeeded Reinhard Heydrich as chief of the *Reichssicherheitshauptamt*, was confronted by his interrogators with a report, attributed to Morgen, of the mass execution in Poniatowa labour camp on 4 November 1943. On the eve of the operation some 15,000 Jews were living in the camp. Most had come from the Warsaw ghetto which had been liquidated in the spring. They had been put to work in the clothing factory of entrepreneur Walter Többens.[9] The report describes how the execution proceeded. The inmates were to undress and lie down in a specially dug pit, then they were executed by a shot in the neck. The next victims had to lie down on top of the corpses and were then executed themselves. 'This went on until the pit was full and the last person dead. Then the pits were filled up.' It was the old system, 'tried and tested', a reference to the method used by the *Einsatzgruppen* at the Eastern front. Morgen noticed that 'none of the victims … had been tortured prior to the executions'. He stated that the mass executions resulted 'in the loss of available labour potential. There were no more people left to operate the machines or to work in the shops. The factories were left with gigantic amounts of raw materials and the managers said that the execution order had come as a complete surprise to them.'

Kaltenbrunner denied all involvement in *Aktion Erntefest* and also claimed not to have known Morgen.[10] During the trial against him in Nuremberg he was no longer confronted with Morgen's statement. As to Morgen himself, it does not seem to have been to his advantage that he probably attended this mass execution, only concluding that the victims had been treated well prior to the execution and that the operation only resulted in a loss of labourers. But assuming he had drafted this report to his superiors, he could hardly vent his possible moral indignation. In all available post-war sources about Morgen, there is no mention whatsoever of the mass execution in Poniatowa, hence many questions remain unanswered; such as was he really present in Poniatowa that day and if so, why?[11] We do know however that Morgen's investigations in the Lublin area did not lead to the prosecution of Christian Wirth. Nevertheless, Morgen claimed in Nuremberg that he would have pursued Wirth 'up to his death'.[12] 'When I heard that Wirth and his command had left Lublin,' Morgen declared, 'I immediately flew there in order to find out whether he was merely transferring his field of activity and would continue elsewhere, but that was not so.'[13] In any case, Wirth's fate was different from that which Morgen had wanted. After having played his part in *Aktion Reinhard*, the 'specialist in mass-destruction of human beings',[14] as Morgen called him, returned to the Adriatic coast where he reportedly was killed fighting partisans on 26 May 1944.[15]

Chapter XIV

A Very Special and Grim Function

In the year he became aware of the extermination of the Jews, Morgen visited Auschwitz concentration camp for the first time, where he also encountered assembly line mass murder. The camp was located in the Polish rural village of Oświęcim in Upper Silesia, some 37 miles west of Krakow. In the spring of 1940 the SS had established the concentration camp on the premises of a former Polish army camp. The first large transport of inmates, consisting of Polish political prisoners, arrived in June 1940. They were housed in the red-brick buildings which had been converted to prison barracks. Inmates passing into the camp did so through the wrought-iron gate bearing the words that were to become notorious: *'Arbeit macht Frei'* (Work sets you free). This slogan, introduced in Dachau by Theodor Eicke, gave inmates only false hope as freedom in Auschwitz did not exist. During the war years the population of the concentration camps made up a labour potential of such importance there could be no question of release. Forced labour was no longer a means to punish prisoners but a goal in itself. The SS provided industry with camp inmates as forced labourers, for which industry had to pay a small compensation to the SS. They hardly cared about the working conditions: when inmates died in the course of their work from exhaustion or an accident, it was considered a cheap way to dispose of unwanted ethnic groups, in particular the Jews. Instead of *Arbeit macht Frei*, the reality was *Vernichtung durch Arbeit* (extermination through labour).

In time, numerous enterprises were set up in the vicinity of Auschwitz. For instance, the German chemistry plant IG Farben started building a factory to make synthetic rubber called Buna in 1941. To house the forced labourers who were deployed in the construction, a new camp was established in the vicinity of the original Camp Auschwitz – the *Stammlager* – which became known as Auschwitz-Monowitz or Auschwitz III. The company paid the SS a compensation for each inmate doing forced labour of 3 RM a day for a non-skilled and 4 RM a day for a skilled worker.

Due to undernourishment, exhausting working conditions and cruel treatment at the hands of the guards, an estimated 35,000 inmates died during the construction of the factory.[1] The factory was not to be finished during the war and not even the smallest piece of rubber was produced. One of the survivors of Monowitz was Italian Primo Levi. 'Definitely dull and grey,' he described the building site. 'This endless maze of iron, concrete, dust and smoke is the denial of beauty. ... Inside the fence, not even a single blade of grass is growing, the earth is saturated with coal and petrol, nothing lives there except machines and slaves and the first more than the latter.'[2]

Ultimately over forty satellite camps would be established around the original Auschwitz concentration camp and over 40,000 inmates were deployed in various industrial enterprises in Upper Silesia. It is estimated that Auschwitz yielded a profit of some 30 million RM to the Nazi state, money earned by providing forced labourers to industry.[3] Today however, Auschwitz is not known for having been a conglomerate of labour camps and industrial enterprises but as the location for mass murder. The first experiments with killing people by gassing were conducted in the *Stammlager* in September 1941. Groups of Soviet prisoners of war and sick inmates were locked into cells in the basement of Block 11, the camp prison, and subsequently pellets of the insecticide *Zyklon-B* were dropped inside. Inhaling the toxic fumes which were emitted proved an effective method of killing numerous people at a time. As it took too long to move the corpses from the cellar in Block 11 to the crematory, that same month a gas chamber was installed in the mortuary of the crematory. Here the *Zyklon-B* pellets were dropped in through apertures in the ceiling.[4]

The experimental gassings in the *Stammlager* preceded the mass murder of Jews in the extermination camps. From the spring of 1942 onwards transports with Jews from all over Europe arrived in Auschwitz almost on a daily basis. As the capacity of the gas chamber in the *Stammlager* was insufficient, a satellite camp was built in the village of Brzezinka (Birkenau in German), located near Oświęcim, which was earmarked to become the centre of mass extermination. This camp, with a surface area of 432 acres and over 300 barracks, came to be known as Auschwitz-Birkenau or Auschwitz II. Eventually four crematory buildings with attached gas chambers would be constructed in Birkenau, raising the murder capacity to 6,000 persons a day.[5] The extermination programme was shaped in an industrial way with a special railway link to the camp, crematories with multiple ovens, gas chambers equipped with a ventilation system and electric elevators for moving the corpses. An estimated 1.1 million people, mostly Jews, were murdered in Auschwitz between March 1942 and November 1944 – the period in which it served as an extermination camp.[6]

As a witness during the Nuremberg trial and the Auschwitz trial in Frankfurt/Main in the 60s, as well as in post war interviews, Morgen reported about his visit to Auschwitz. As to the occasion of his investigation in Auschwitz he always declared the same: it started with a field post parcel that was confiscated by Customs. Someone with a *Sanitätsdienstgrad* (medical rank) had sent it from Auschwitz to his wife in Germany. The parcel would never arrive though, because during a routine check it was opened by Customs officers who discovered it contained chunks of gold. It was confiscated as contraband and reported to the responsible *SS- und Polizeigericht*. That is how Morgen got involved in the case. He established that it was 'high carat dental gold, melted down in a primitive way', as he declared in Frankfurt. 'There was one large chunk, maybe the size of two fists, the other was considerably smaller, the third even more insignificant. Yet, all told, a fair number of pounds was concerned.'

Initially he was puzzled how careless the sender had been at his work. 'It seemed a clear case of stupidity. However, the longer I thought about it, the more I believed I had underestimated the sender. Look at it this way: amongst the hundreds of thousands of parcels, the chance of this dangerous delivery being spotted and confiscated was extremely small. A rather shifty primitivity and unscrupulous recklessness seemed to me to predominate in this perpetrator, which would prove correct during my later investigation in Auschwitz.'

Morgen knew about 'the dental teams in the concentration camps having orders to collect all gold after cremations and hand it over to the *Reichsbank*'. But in his declaration in Frankfurt he made it look like he was amazed and shocked by the large amount of dental gold. He declared he had estimated at the time how many fillings – and so deaths – had been required for this large amount of gold. Since a gold filling weighs only a few ounces, he established that to collect such an amount of gold, 'numerous people' would have to be killed. But while not everybody wore gold fillings, actually it would have to be many, many more deaths. He calculated that if 'each 20th, 50th or 100th prisoner wore gold fillings, the confiscated amount was equal to 20, 50 or 100,000 corpses. He found it a shocking thought but claimed the most incomprehensible thing for him was that 'the executor had been able to collect such amounts unnoticed'. 50,000 or 100,000 people had disappeared and that, in his opinion, could 'not be the result of natural causes of death, so these people had to have been murdered here'. Only then would it have dawned on him that 'this hardly known Auschwitz – of which I could only find the geographical location on a map with some difficulty – was one of the largest locations of mass extermination of people the world has ever seen'.[7]

But did Morgen really not know prior to his visit to Auschwitz that large numbers of Jews were murdered there, as he claimed in Frankfurt? That contradicts his earlier statement in Nuremberg in which he told of his visit to Christian Wirth which had taken place before his visit to Auschwitz. At that time, Morgen saw with his own eyes the enormous number of valuables which had been taken away from the Jews and an oven for melting down the gold. According to Morgen, Wirth reported not only in detail about the extermination programme but he also told him about Auschwitz and camp commander Rudolph Höss.[8] In an interview for the British documentary *World at War* (1973–4) he stated that it had been explained to him in advance that 'Auschwitz-Birkenau concentration camp served a very special and grim purpose: the extermination of the Jews – the so-called *Endlösung* as Hitler called his definite solution'.[9] Before he visited the camp, he was already far better informed about the genocide taking place in Auschwitz than he pretended in Frankfurt. In view of his work, it is most logical to say: it is unlikely that, after all his visits to concentration camps where he contacted SS men who had been involved in the extermination camps, he knew nothing at all about the extermination programme. His testimony, quoted in the next chapter, leads one to assume that he certainly did know what was happening in Auschwitz.

Chapter XV

A Guided Tour of the Extermination Factory

One day in the autumn of 1943, Konrad Morgen, who had been promoted to *SS-Hauptsturmführer* on 9 November 1943,[1] set off in the direction of Auschwitz to see what was happening in this secretive place. After a journey by train he arrived at the station of the small Polish town. He was puzzled by the undistinguished view. 'One way or another, you would expect that a site where such grim things were happening on such an immense scale would make an extremely frightening impression, that there would be something sinister about it. But no, Auschwitz was a quite normal grey and sorry looking small industrial town. Everything looked normal and nothing could be seen of the concentration camp either.'[2]

During the Auschwitz trial in Frankfurt he also stated he had expected a 'special atmosphere' on arrival. He said he 'remained standing in the station for some time, to see something somewhere. But Auschwitz was a small town with a very large transit and shunting yard, something like Bebra – a city in central Germany and an important rail junction. Trains were passing through, one after the other: troop transports to the east, transports returning with the injured, trains carrying coal, ore, goods and persons as well. People got off them, the young lively, the elder grumping and exhausted, as if it were the most normal thing in the world. I saw transports of prisoners in their striped uniforms as well. But they all left, not one of them stayed.'

He was picked up at the station and driven to the camp in a staff car. Seen from the outside the camp did not make a special impression on him. It was a sight 'you would expect of a prisoners of war camp or other concentration camps: high walls, barbed wire, watch towers, and guards walking about. A gate, activity by inmates but nothing out of the ordinary.'[3] On arrival he reported to the camp commander, *SS-Obersturmbannführer* Rudolph Höss. 'This Höss was one of the strangest people I ever met,' Morgen recalled after the war. 'I can perhaps best describe him as a man hewn out of solid granite because he hardly moved and never showed any emotion. He spoke very slowly and softly, ponderously and measured.¹⁴ The camp commander told him, 'He had been given an unusually grim task and not everybody's character was up to it,'⁵ by which he meant the extermination of the Jews. Prior to his appointment in Auschwitz and his involvement in the extermination programme he had gained experience in other concentration camps from 1934 onwards. Hence he was an old hand in the trade and, moreover, he was a National Socialist of the early days.

Rudolph Höss was born 25 November 1900 in Baden-Baden. He had fought at the front in Turkey as a teenager during the First World War. After the war he was active in a *Freikorps* and he joined the NSDAP in 1922. He took part in the resistance against the French when they occupied the Ruhr area in 1923. Together with Hitler's future private secretary Martin Bormann, he was involved in the manslaughter of a communist teacher who was suspected of having betrayed a National Socialist to the French. Although Höss denied having been the prime executor himself, he was sentenced as such to ten years imprisonment. As a result of the amnesty law of 14 July 1928 he was released after serving less than half of his time. In the years to follow, he no longer wished to occupy himself with political struggle but wanted to start life as a farmer. He joined the *Artamanen Brüderschaft* which strove for colonization of the east by young German farmers. Himmler was a member of this brotherhood as well. About his dream of being a farmer, Höss wrote in his memoirs: 'Only one goal existed for me, which justified striving and fighting for – a farmhouse, which I had earned by hard work, with a large and healthy family. That was to become the content of my life, my ultimate goal.'⁶

Höss got married and had five children but in 1934 he took a direction which would lead him to a future very different from that of a farmer. He joined the SS and was placed in Dachau concentration camp, where he gained experience in the concentration camp system. In his memoirs he wrote he had trouble imposing the cruel policy of camp commander Eicke. Being a former prisoner himself, he felt 'too much attracted to the inmates inwardly, as for years I had shared their lives, their needs'. At the same time however, he was 'convinced of the necessity of a concentration camp'. He wrote: 'True enemies of the state should certainly be imprisoned, anti-socials and professional criminals deprived of their freedom in order to protect society against their evil influence. … But I certainly disagreed with Eicke's attitude towards inmates, deliberately stirring up the lowest feelings of hatred amongst the guards with his policy towards personnel, granting subordinates authority over inmates and letting subordinates, even absolutely incompetent guards, keep their jobs.'[7] Seemingly against grudge, sadism and high-handedness, but ideologically convinced of the necessity of the concentration camps, he was in relation to Himmler's view the ideal camp officer.

After having been employed in Dachau as *Blockführer* – in charge of a camp block – and *Rapportführer* – responsible for the frequent counting of inmates – he rose to *Schutzhaftlagerführer* in Sachsenhausen in 1938. In the spring of 1940, Himmler transferred him to Auschwitz as camp commander in order to establish the concentration camp. Despite his criticism of the cruel policy of his mentor Theodor Eicke, Auschwitz was modelled after Dachau, including the system of 'divide and rule' whereby convicted criminals or political prisoners were appointed as kapos to oversee other inmates, often resulting in abuse of authority. In his memoirs, Höss blamed his subordinates for copying Eicke's system. 'They did not believe my continuing admonitions that Eicke's views had become obsolete due to the changes in the concentration camps. They could not get Eicke's lessons out of their system.'[8] He felt misunderstood and unassisted by his men. Disappointed, he turned inward and grabbed the bottle for courage.[9]

Was Höss just a soft-hearted man who had accidently landed in the wrong spot? He wanted to make others believe so. But that same Höss was an obedient exterminator of the Jews. In his memoirs he wrote that high-ranking visitors to the camp asked him time and again how he and his men could 'continuously watch these events, how did we cope? I always answered that by saying that all human feelings had to be set aside against the iron consistency with which we had to obey the *Führer's* orders.' He complained about the gruesome scenes he had to watch. Once he witnessed a bitterly crying mother being sent into the gas chamber with her children. 'Out of sheer pity, I would have preferred to have left the scene – but I was not to display the slightest emotion. I had to watch everything. I had to be present, day and night at the removal, the cremation of the corpses, the extraction of teeth, the cutting of hair, I had to watch all those horrors for hours. ... I had to do all of this ... as I had to show I not only gave the orders and set the rules, but was willing to attend everything everywhere, as I demanded the same of my subordinates.'[10]

His commiserations stemmed more from self-pity than from moral indignation about the mass murder of the Jews. In his view, orders from the *Führer* were to be obeyed unconditionally. While these horrors occurred in his camp, Höss made a fuss over details. One of his rules was: 'The newly laid gardens are the jewels of the camp. It must go without saying for all SS men to leave the gardens alone and not to step onto the flower beds.'[11] The image of Höss that emerges is that of a bureaucrat, loyal to the Nazi ideology and the *Führer*, who followed the orders given to him as accurately as possible but experienced no great satisfaction while doing so. As to his nature, he differed from people like Karl Koch and Christian Wirth who seemed to enjoy themselves hugely within the system of terror and destruction. This however did not mitigate Höss's guilt in any way.

After Morgen and Höss had made their acquaintance, an officer was allotted to him with orders to guide him through the camp. Subsequently they visited all important sections of the camp by car, including the extermination camp in Birkenau. During the Auschwitz trial in Frankfurt, Morgen reported extensively about this guided tour of the camp. He told that the tour started at the 'beginning of the end', the platform of Birkenau. There the procedure when a new transport arrived was explained to him. The platform was ringed by guards and when the doors of the carriages were opened the Jews had to disembark and leave their baggage behind. Men and women were separated and 'rabbis and equally prominent Jewish persons ... were taken aside immediately'. According to his guide, it was 'expected of these prominent persons to send as many post cards and letters as possible with greetings all over the world in order to obscure any suspicion that something gruesome was taking place here'. Such mail, preprinted postcards with soothing words, were actually sent, from the fictitious village of Waldsee to next of kin, to reassure those Jews still to be deported to the East.

After men and women had been separated they were asked if there were skilled people who could be useful to the industry connected to the camp. Those specialists, like engineers, technicians and such, were singled out while the rest were checked to see if they were fit for labour. Those who were and the skilled prisoners were marched off to the prison camp of Birkenau where in the course of time many would perish as a result of the deplorable living situation and the inhuman work conditions. Prisoners unfit for labour, like children, the elderly, the sick, the disabled, immediately left for the gas chambers, most of them on foot, the more or less disabled by truck. Morgen's guide told him that 'when there was no time, no physician available or there were simply too many prisoners, the procedure was sometimes cut short: the arrivals were told, in polite words, that the camp was a few miles away and that those feeling too sick or too weak or for whom walking was too uncomfortable could make use of a vehicle already waiting for them. There was a stampede to get into the vehicles. Those who didn't get in could march into the camp, while the others had unknowingly opted for death.'

After having seen the platform, Morgen and his guide visited Birkenau itself. 'From the outside, nothing conspicuous could be seen either: large, somewhat crooked gates with sentries,' he recalled. He was shown 'Canada', the part of the camp where the baggage of the deported Jews was collected and sorted to be sent to Germany to be reused. Morgen saw 'from the last transports stacks of suitcases broken open, laundry, brief cases, but also complete dental equipment, shoemakers' tools and medicine kits lying around. Obviously the so-called evacuees had actually assumed they would be resettled in the East, as they had been told and had prepared themselves accordingly.' The department took its name from the large amount of stored goods, associated with the wealth and abundance of Canada.

In Birkenau, Morgen was also shown what he, as he said, had come to see: a crematory and a gas chamber. Based on the details he described he probably visited Krema II or III, two T-shaped crematories, one a mirror image of the other, built in 1943. In Frankfurt he gave a detailed description of what such a building looked like. 'They were one storey spaces with gabled roofs that could just as well have been sheds or small workshops. Even the very wide and massive chimneys would not be noticed by lays as they were quite modest, they ended just above the roofs.' At that moment there was no gassing in progress but he did see 'a herd … of Jewish inmates with their yellow star and their kapo carrying a long cudgel … . They, the kapos, continuously walked around them, yelling orders and catching every look. It crossed my mind they were behaving exactly like shepherds and their herds. I told my guide, he laughed about it and said: "they have been ordered to". The victims who were going to be killed had to be put at ease by the "brothers in faith", acting as kapos.' Kapos were instructed 'not to beat the arrivals. An outbreak of panic had to be avoided. They should give them a little fear and respect, for the rest just be there and guide them to the location where the camp management wanted them.'

'Where they wanted them' was the gas chamber. Before entering this chamber, the victims were to undress in a room which, according to Morgen, was comparable to a dressing room in a gym. 'There were simple wooden benches with racks for clothing and, conspicuously, each place was numbered, had a cloakroom number. It was also pointed out to the victims they had to watch their clothing, they should remember their number, everything aimed at keeping up the façade, literally until the last second, so as not to arouse even the slightest suspicion and let the victims walk unexpectedly into the trap.'

Morgen stated that he visited the gas chamber as well. The victims were guided there by 'a large arrow pointing to a corridor with the short text: "to the showers" in six or seven languages. They were also told: you will undress, take a shower and be disinfected. The corridor led to various rooms without any furnishing: barren, empty, concrete floors. Conspicuous and moreover unexplainable was a shaft of latticework in the centre of the room reaching up to the ceiling. I had no explanation for this until I was told that gas in crystalline form, *Zyklon-B* pellets, was dropped into the chamber through an aperture in the roof. Until that moment, the victims were completely ignorant, but then of course, it was too late.'

After the victims had been gassed, the corpses were taken to the ground floor in an elevator (the gas chambers of Krema II and III were located in the basement) and then to the crematory which was also shown to Morgen. He described it as 'an enormous hall with the ovens at one end in a long row, with a flat floor; everything exhaled a businesslike, neutral and technical atmosphere. It was all shining like a mirror, polished, and some inmates dressed as mechanics were cleaning their equipment with robotlike movements. As for the rest, it was quiet and empty.'

Morgen recalled he had not seen a single SS man in the crematory. He would however very much like to see 'the SS men and get to know them, who are running and managing this whole system'. Hence, a visit was paid the to the guards' quarters in Birkenau. This visit made a shocking impression on Morgen. The housing was very different from what he was used to in military barracks which in general 'were characterized in all armies of the world by a Spartan simplicity'. While expecting a tidy room with a desk, posters and bunks, he entered a 'somewhat shadowy room'. 'Ranged in a circle was a weird collection of benches. On these benches a few SS men lay, most of them without an officer's rank, staring at infinity, their eyes glassy.' Morgen had the impression 'they must have consumed quite a lot of alcohol the previous night'. But what stunned him the most was 'that instead of a desk, there was a large furnace in the room and four or five young girls were baking potato cookies. They were obviously Jewish, very pretty, Oriental beauties, big breasted, sparkling eyes. They did not wear prison garb but normal, rather sexy civilian clothing. And they took those cookies to their pashas dozing on the benches, asking them if there was enough sugar on the cookies and feeding them.'

No one paid any attention to the visitors, even though Morgen's guide was higher in rank than the others. 'Nobody said a word and no one could be disturbed. And I could not believe my ears, these female inmates and the SS men were on first name terms. I must have looked quite astonishedly at my guide. He just shrugged his shoulders and said: "The men have a busy night under their belts. They have processed a few transports." ... That also meant that during the night while I was travelling to Auschwitz by train, a few thousand people, a few trainloads, had been gassed and cremated here. And of all these thousands of people not the tiniest speck of dust had been left behind in the ovens.'

After this disheartening experience for Morgen, the tour was resumed through the rest of the camp. He was shown a prisoners' barracks, cultural things and a hospital ward. He also was shown the Bunker – the camp prison – in the *Stammlager*. There he was shown, quite openly and willingly, the so-called black wall where the executions took place. Late afternoon the tour came to an end and it was time for action. Morgen had the entire SS camp staff fall in in their quarters. They were ordered to stand in front of their lockers which were to be investigated by Morgen. As expected, he discovered all sorts of suspicious articles: 'gold rings, coins, necklaces, pearls, currency from all over the world. In one locker a few "souvenirs" only, in others a small fortune.' One of the lockers contained a strange item: 'the testicles of a recently slaughtered bull. The owner of the locker blushed and explained those were used to enhance one's own sexual potency.' After this first round of inspection, Morgen's working day was over and he went to his assigned quarters to spend the night.[12]

Chapter XVI

A Cosy Life for the SS in Auschwitz

T he storage shed of the SS in Auschwitz was a treasure trove for inmates like Slovakian Jew Rudolf Vrba. His testimony reveals the enormous scale of corruption in the camp. He was imprisoned from 30 June 1942 until 10 April 1944 and was temporarily employed in this depot where, in his words, 'mountains of food were stored', so the guards were not in want of anything. While the common German on the home front had to scrape his meagre ration together with ration cards, the kitchen for the camp staff had plentiful supplies of tinned meat, vegetables, fruit and jam at its disposal and 'bottles of mineral water, neatly stacked in endless rows'.[1] A kapo named Franz was in charge of the depot. He often smuggled food into the camp where it was a valuable medium of exchange. With food you could buy protection for you and yourself from influential inmates. Only prisoners with good contacts within the so-called camp aristocracy had any chance of survival. Theft, black marketeering and bribery formed part and parcel of daily camp life. Guards as well as inmates were guilty of it on a massive scale.

Vrba also owed his life to the flourishing corruption in the camp. Franz never forgot to reward his labourers for their services, and from time to time he dropped a jar of jam or pickles so they could consume it immediately. For the undernourished prisoners, eating off the floor was no problem at all. The kapo also looked the other way when Vrba and his colleagues stole a bottle of mineral water, as long as they did it unnoticed so the SS would not find out. In the heavily guarded depot it was impossible however to prevent the SS from noticing that items were missing. Security was tightened and from then on Franz and his colleagues were frisked before leaving the warehouse. After a box of marmalade had been stolen, Franz was relieved of his function, incarcerated in the bunker and subsequently transferred to a penal unit. His coworkers, including Vrba, were also fired. Vrba landed in Monowitz where he managed to survive thanks to a French civilian worker who took him under his wing.

Only after his transfer to 'Canada' Vrba discovered how Auschwitz operated as a collection centre for valuables from all over Europe. He saw how hundreds of inmates in this 'warehouse of body snatchers' were toiling to sort clothing, foodstuffs and other possessions of the victims to be reused or to line the coffers of the State. Vrba saw a 'gigantic mountain of suitcases, rucksacks, bags and parcels' and 'hundreds of prams. Shining prams, suitable for a first-born. Worn down prams that had been used by subsequent generations. Luxurious, showy prams, veritable status symbols and modest and simple prams for those possessing neither money nor status.'[2] Gradually it dawned on him that the former owners of these items had all been murdered. 'Slowly but surely, the bags, the clothing, the food and the sad pictures became people to me, prams became babies and the heaps of carefully sorted shoes became children, just like my niece.'[3]

In 'Canada' inmates also stole goods, on a far larger scale than in the SS depots, as the huge number of articles made meticulous registering of items impossible. Despite frequent frisking by guards and the threat of beatings – or worse – inmates deployed in 'Canada' managed to 'organize' sufficient food for themselves. On his first day, Vrba watched his mates unveil the booty: 'One of them had six tins of sardines, another two pounds of figs. Shirts, fruit, soap, salami, sausages and ham were on display until the barracks looked like a well-stocked supermarket.'[4]

Vrba also became adept at gathering food. Whenever he climbed into a car to unload the baggage left behind, he knew exactly which suitcase contained which food. 'I learned, we all learned, to distinguish various transports containing various sorts of food. A train from Greece meant a banquet of figs and olives; from France, possibly sardines; from Slovakia salami and tasty, homemade black bread.' Frequently this food was consumed immediately, inside a car and out of sight of the guards. 'It seemed heartless maybe, almost inhuman, to steal food when its owners were being herded to their death by the thousands,' so Vrba said, 'but there was absolutely nothing we could do to help them.'[5] For prisoners like him, stealing of food was a means to survive. It was due to the stolen food, his privileged position and his relationship with the 'camp aristocracy' that he survived Auschwitz and had gathered sufficient physical and mental strength to escape from the camp on 10 April 1944.

The inmates lived in conditions diametrically opposed to those of the SS guards: to the latter, Auschwitz was all but a holiday resort. The most gruesome tasks, removing the corpses from the gas chambers and cremating them, was left to Jewish prisoners who were put to work in the so-called *Sonderkommandos*. While their comrades suffered hardships on the Eastern front, the men in Auschwitz lived like kings. *SS-Rottenführer* Oskar Gröning talked extensively with British producer and author Laurence Rees about his life in the camp. In Auschwitz, Gröning was responsible for sorting and counting all the different currencies taken away from the deported Jews. He told Rees that he and his colleagues drank much alcohol that they found in the baggage of their victims. 'We weren't drunk every day – but it happened,' he told him. 'We went to bed drunk and when someone was too miserable to turn out the light, he just shot the bulb away and no one said anything about it.' He described the main camp of Auschwitz 'as a small town. There was gossip, there was a vegetable store where you could purchase beans to make soup. There was a canteen, a cinema, a theatre with professional performances. There was a sporting club of which I was a member. There was dancing – more than enough fun and games.'[6]

While their prisoners were housed in filthy, draughty sheds, the camp guards were billeted in comfortable barracks. Officers and their families were housed in confiscated houses in the vicinity of the camp. The Höss family also lived in the vicinity of the camp where they fully enjoyed themselves. 'Each wish my wife or my kids fostered was fulfilled. ... My wife owned a paradise of flowers. ... The children kept all sorts of strange animals in the garden all the time ... . Or in summer they were frolicking in the pond in the garden or in the river Sola.'[7]

In January 2007 a photo album which once had belonged to *SS-Obersturmführer* Karl-Friedrich Höcker, adjutant of *SS-Sturmbannführer* Richard Baer who was commander of *Stammlager* Auschwitz from May 1944, was donated to the United States Holocaust Memorial Museum in Washington D.C. The pictures from the summer and autumn of 1944 provide a tarnished view on the relaxed life of camp personnel in Auschwitz. They show SS men eating and drinking in a pleasant atmosphere, how they enjoyed themselves with an accordion and with women, mainly female camp guards. One can see how a hunting trip is made and an excursion to a coal mine. Numerous pictures have been taken at the Solahütte, a rustic holiday resort for SS camp personnel some 18 miles from Auschwitz. Camp guards who had performed their duties extremely well, for instance having prevented an attempt at escaping, were rewarded with a stay of a few days in this rest home in the forest. Apart from Rudolph Höss, notorious camp doctor Joseph Mengele and Joseph Kramer, future commander of Bergen-Belsen, were captured on photo in a relaxed atmosphere.[8]

Knowing that in the period these pictures were taken the extermination factory in Birkenau was operating at full capacity, gives these pictures a gruesome dimension. In March 1944 the Germans had invaded Hungary, and from 14 May onwards trains carrying Jews departed daily in the direction of Auschwitz. Within eight weeks the Nazis succeeded in deporting 438,000 Hungarian Jews to the camp. Most of them – 394,000 – were gassed on arrival. The crematories could not keep up with the flood so the remainder had to be cremated in open pits.[9]

But despite the comfortable life the camp personnel enjoyed, the large amount of valuables taken to the camp by the deported Jews were a temptation many guards could not resist. That Morgen, on day one of his investigation in Auschwitz, discovered so much evidence of thievery by guards showed the character of the morality within the camp. That, however, was well-known to the SS management before his arrival. Rudolf Vrba wrote that *SS-Standartenführer* Rudolf Mildner, chief of the *Gestapo* in Katowice, launched an investigation in Auschwitz as early as December 1942 into 'rumours … that the SS was smuggling gold, jewellery and money out of the camp'. Vrba presumed the rumours were based on fact and 'assumed that leaders of the underground [the resistance movement in the camp, organized by inmates] were stealing sizable amounts of gold, jewellery and money, not to enrich themselves but to bribe their guards'.[10]

Guards did have other means to convert valuable items to their own use. According to *SS-Rottenführer* Perry Broad, employed in the *Politische Abteilung* (political department) of the camp from June 1942 onwards, large amounts of money 'were lying on the roads in Birkenau waiting to be picked up; carelessly thrown away by inmates on their way from the platform to the camp or from the trucks during the ride to the gas chambers. Most guards who found it could not resist the temptation and did not take everything back to the department for valuables or kept all of it, despite the risk of severe penalties.' According to Broad, a lively black trade emerged in and around the camp. 'In the station, shady railway workers and profiteers could sell any amount of vodka to you. The black marketeers made huge profits. They could sell their merchandise for payment in gold dollars, rubles or Reichsmarks. Their customers possessed an abundance of various currencies.'

Broad claimed 'one of the money stores of the section which looked after the valuables' had even been broken into. 'Considering the immense number of coffers containing uncounted money, it proved to be quite impossible to tell how many of these had been taken, and even less possible to find out what amount of money had been stolen by the burglar.'[11] Camp commander Höss wrote that in particular many valuables entered the camp on transports of Jews from the west. He mentioned: 'gemstones worth millions, watches studded with diamonds, watches made of gold and platinum of inestimable value, coins from all countries'. All of these valuables were to be transferred in boxes to the *SS-Wirtschafts und Verwaltungshauptamt* in Berlin and subsequently be deposited in the *Reichsbank*. But a considerable part of these valuables never ended up there, but disappeared into the pockets of the SS, even Höss had to acknowledge. 'In the camp itself, these valuable items of the Jews caused grave problems. It was demoralizing for the members of the SS who weren't always strong enough to resist the temptation. Even the death penalty and the longest prison terms were not sufficiently prohibitive.'

Höss was also aware that stolen valuables were being used by inmates to bribe guards. He declared: 'For inmates, these valuables from the Jews offered an abundance of possibilities. Most attempts at escape are connected with this. With the money ... or with watches, rings and such, all sorts of things were bought from the SS or civilian labourers. Alcohol, tobacco, foodstuffs, forged papers, weapons and ammunition were quite common. In Birkenau, men forced entry into the women's camp at night, they even bribed a few guides. ... Those in possession of money or jewellery were able to buy better work, buy the friendship of kapos and *Blockältesten* or even a permanent stay in the hospital ward with excellent treatment. Despite the tightest security, these conditions could not be improved. The Jew gold became a catastrophe for the camp.'[12]

Chapter XVII

'Class justice' in Auschwitz

Konrad Morgen's investigation in Auschwitz was at least as large in scale as the big corruption case in Buchenwald. Over a period of about six months research was conducted in Auschwitz into evidence of thievery and other crimes committed by personnel of the camp. In this, Morgen was assisted by his colleagues: judges *SS-Hauptsturmführer* Helmut Bartsch, *SS-Obersturmführer* Wilhelm Reimers and *SS-Untersturmführer* Gerhard Wiebeck. *SS-Hauptsturmführer* Heinz Drescher also visited the camp in connection with this investigation. He was not a judge but chief of the department of person identification and fingerprint registration of the *Reichspolizeikriminalamt* of the RSHA.[1] As appears from Morgen's testimony in Frankfurt, inspection of lockers was part of the investigation. According to *SS-Oberscharführer* Wilhelm Claussen, who was employed in the political department in Auschwitz, the lockers of the SS men lower in rank were inspected in particular. In his opinion, officers and SS men in responsible positions were granted 'a lot of time to hide their treasures or send them out of the camp'. Claussen found this all the more remarkable as, in his opinion, these prominent persons had the most to conceal.[2] The lockers of lower-ranking and less important SS men proved to contain enough booty however, ranging from valuables to daily utensils and foodstuffs.

Oskar Gröning was lucky enough to be in Berlin at the time the lockers were being inspected. After the war he declared that to his colleagues 'the moment Morgen entered the subaltern officers' quarters, it came as a complete surprise.' When Gröning returned to the camp he found out that two of his comrades had been arrested and imprisoned. 'In one of the lockers, fountain pens and a tin of sardines were found and I don't know what they found in the other guy's locker, but he hanged himself a little later.' Gröning's locker was sealed and would only be opened in his presence. When he returned from Berlin, he and his mates managed to pull the cupboard forward, remove the plywood back and 'take out the suspicious bars of soap and toothpaste' prior to the inspection. After having shoved the cupboards back in place, the inspectors were called in. They removed the seal, opened the cupboard and established that nothing suspicious was hidden inside. Gröning got off unscathed and was not arrested, but that did not apply to many of his colleagues. After the war Morgen declared that 'the conduct of the SS in Auschwitz did not in any way match the standards one may expect from soldiers. They made the impression of demoralized, animal-like parasites.'[3]

According to SS judge Helmut Bartsch, 123 investigations into SS men in Auschwitz were conducted between October 1943 and April 1944. 'On the basis of its findings,' he claimed, 'twenty-three lower-ranking and two higher-ranking SS leaders were arrested.' The penalties varied between two and four years imprisonment, 'and in most cases the convicts were discharged from the *Waffen-SS*.'[4] One of the high-ranking SS officers Bartsch meant was probably *SS-Untersturmführer* Maximilian Grabner. He and his associate *SS-Oberscharführer* Wilhelm Boger were, in Morgen's opinion, among the cruellest guards in Auschwitz and he charged them with illegal murder.[5] Both men were employed in the political department of Auschwitz. Each concentration camp had such a department which was officially designated *Abteilung II*. The department acted independently from the camp commander and was a branch of the *Gestapo* – the reason it was also known as Camp *Gestapo*. The section handled the allocation of inmates and entered fresh arrivals in the prison records. In addition, workers in this branch occupied themselves with interrogating, punishing and executing prisoners who had committed a violation. Grabner and Boger earned their notoriety from these tasks.

Wilhelm Boger, born in 1906, had been active in Auschwitz since December 1942. He invented a cruel torture tool that came to be known as the 'Boger swing'. The construction looked like a revolving spit and a prisoner was tied to it. The 'spit', an iron bar, was positioned behind the knees of the victim, then his hands were tied around his bended knees. The iron bar was then turned until the victim was hanging upside down with his buttocks up. While Boger's victims remained in this painful position for a long time, he interrogated them. As if the torture wasn't cruel enough, Boger beat their genitals with a bat to force a confession out of them.[6]

Morgen and his colleagues failed to take the beastly Boger to court. He remained active in Auschwitz until the evacuation of the camp in January 1945. He was then transferred to Mittelbau concentration camp where he was again employed as an official in the political department.[7] Morgen and his colleagues did succeed in opening a case against Boger's superior Maximilian Grabner though. This former police officer, born in Vienna in 1905, was initially employed in the *Gestapo* office in Katowice but was transferred to concentration camp Auschwitz in May 1940. There he was put in charge of the political department. His former colleague Perry Broad described him as 'the most outstanding man in Auschwitz thanks to his unscrupulous brutality, his morbid ambition, his need for self-assertion and his proverbial double dealing. Even the commander … avoided, wherever he could, disputes with this experienced *Gestapo*-man.'[8]

While he, as chief of the camp *Gestapo*, was supposed to fight corruption among the camp guards, he was guilty of it himself. Feliks Mylyk, a former prisoner who was employed in the political department, testified after the war that he had had to 'organize various things' for Grabner. 'In his Auschwitz apartment I saw many suitcases, coats and other items from "Canada",' he declared. 'The suitcases still bore the names of their former rightful owners.' Items from 'Canada' were packed by Mylyk and sent to Grabner's family in Vienna. According to Perry Broad, various kapos delivered stolen goods to Grabner including furniture and food. In exchange he wrote favourable reports about them.[9]

The site where Grabner and Boger committed most of their crimes was the Bunker, the camp prison located in Block 11 in the *Stammlager*. Inmates often remained here for months in small filthy cells where they were tortured, became severely undernourished or froze to death in winter. Grabner performed a regular 'cleaning up' when inmates were executed against the wall between Block 10 and 11, better known as the black wall. Among the executed were inmates who had been caught stealing, who had been caught during an escape attempt or hadn't revealed enough information under torture. Being of Jewish ancestry or being a priest sometimes was enough reason to be killed. In Nuremberg, Morgen testified he had stumbled onto Grabner's track following a conversation with a camp doctor. He told Morgen that Grabner had ordered the doctor to kill pregnant Polish women but he had refused.[10] On further investigation the 'illegal' executions by Grabner and his associates were unveiled. According to Morgen they had done so on their own initiative; 'they were not ordered to do so, and they did not give notices of death to their bosses.'[11] In Morgen's view illegal murder was evident and he had Grabner arrested in December 1943 on suspicion of murder and thievery.[12]

Following Grabner's arrest, Morgen had a conflict with Heinrich Müller, the chief of the *Gestapo* and thus Grabner's superior. Morgen explained this during the Auschwitz trial in Frankfurt. He claimed to have been summoned to Berlin by Müller. Müller had pointed out to him that he had exceeded his authority after which Morgen told the *Gestapo* chief, 'We still live in a constitutional state and there are limits which even the *Gestapo* has to adhere to.' Müller would have become extremely angry and kicked Morgen out of his office. After Müller had calmed down, Morgen returned and the following dialogue reportedly took place:

Morgen: Herr Müller, isn't it the Führer, and you, the chief of the Gestapo, who have the ultimate decision on every sentence?

Müller: Yes.

Morgen: Well, how would you judge it, if someone went far beyond your orders, and without informing you, through his own decision, killed a hard-working prisoner?

Müller: That's impossible, that just doesn't happen!

Morgen: You see, Lieutenant General, Sir, that is how people are ignoring your authority in the camps, that is what Grabner did, and that is why I arrested him.

Müller: Well, this is very different, this I understand.[13]

Whether Morgen actually confronted the powerful *Gestapo* chief in this way cannot be verified as no minutes were taken and no declarations exist of witnesses present at the conversation. Whether or not it was due to Morgen's plea in Müller's office, the trial against Grabner proceeded for the time being. It was held in October 1944 in Weimar, shortly after the first trial against Koch. The court was chaired by Dr Werner Hansen. He explained afterwards that Grabner had been indicted for the murder of 2,000 inmates who would have been shot to make space in the overcrowded camp prison in Auschwitz. Grabner denied he had acted on his own accord; he would have had permission from the RSHA. When inquiries were send to the RSHA, a reaction was not forthcoming. Camp commander Höss backed up Grabner but accepted no responsibility for the executions which had taken place near the Bunker. Wilhelm Boger was also subpoenaed in the case against his boss. According to SS judge Wiebeck, he defended his boss with the words: 'We killed hardly enough of them. Everything was done in the name of the *Führer* and the *Reich*.' Boger called Grabner a scapegoat who would hang instead of the bigwigs. He described Morgen as 'the henchman of the top leaders'.[14]

The prosecution demanded twelve years imprisonment for Grabner, but the case was postponed to delve further into the question of whether the RSHA had ordered the execution of inmates or not. As Müller obstructed this, the case ground to a halt. Eventually Grabner returned to Katowice where he had worked before he was transferred to Auschwitz. After the war a Polish tribunal in Krakow sentenced him to death on 22 December 1947 and he was executed.[15] Investigations by Morgen's commission into other staff members of Auschwitz bogged down too. After gold had been discovered in his possessions, *SS-Oberscharführer* Wilhelm Emmerich, who was employed in *Aussenkommando* Chelmek, a satellite camp of Auschwitz where shoes were produced, was arrested. He was released however without a trial having been held against him. Mainly the higher-ranking SS officers were spared, enhancing the impression of class justice. Efforts by Morgen and his team to take *SS-Hauptsturmführer* Heinrich Schwarz and *SS-Sturmbannführer* Hans Aumeier failed as well.[16] The first named was commander of Auschwitz-Monowitz and the latter the former *Schutzhaftlagerführer* in *Stammlager* Auschwitz and had been transferred by Höss on suspicion of corruption as early as August 1943.[17] The attempt to prosecute the most important man in Auschwitz, camp commander Höss, was equally unsuccessful.

Chapter XVIII

The Secret Love of the Camp Commander

During his investigation in Auschwitz, Morgen discovered Rudolph Höss had a secret relationship with a female prisoner. It was an informant, *SS-Hauptscharführer* Gerhard Palitzsch, since 1940 *Rapportführer* in Auschwitz, who informed him of it.[1] The prisoner was named Eleonore Hodys, born in Vienna in 1903 and a physician. She had arrived in Auschwitz from concentration camp Ravensbrück on one of the first transports of women.[2] As she was a political prisoner of Aryan descent she was put to work in the villa of the Höss family, she declared during an interrogation by Morgen in the autumn of 1944. She 'liked working in the house of the commander. ... I was given food. Alone in my room, I had the same food as the commander himself. ... It was very good and could easily be compared to the menu of a large hotel in peacetime.'

Soon the commander developed a 'special interest' in her. When she was not in his house he visited her elsewhere and talked about his work. She had to admit, she 'liked him as a man'. To show his affection, the commander granted her all sorts of privileges, including her own quarters in Block 4 she could decorate with furniture and tapestries. She claimed she even had a cook at her disposal and a maid and that a party was organized in the house of the commander on her birthday. Things went so far that other prisoners thought she was one of Höss's relatives. At some moment in time, according to Hodys in May 1942, Höss attempted to seduce his favourite prisoner when his wife was absent. He kissed her, but Hodys made it abundantly clear she would have nothing of it. 'I was surprised and afraid, I fled and locked myself inside the bathroom. There were too many obstacles between him and me in regard to his position and the fact that he was married. From that moment on I never entered the house of the commander again. I reported sick and tried to hide from him whenever he asked for me.'

It is likely that Höss's wife had got wind of the overtures her husband had made towards Hodys; in any case she was, in her own words, fired as a seamstress in September and landed in a penal company. Despite having been promised work in the camp hospital, on 16 October 1942 she landed in the *Kommandanturarrest*, better known as the Bunker. Compared to most other prisoners she still did not want for anything. 'Until January 1943, I was doing rather well in the *Kommandanturarrest*. Usually I had a single cell with a good bed and a mattress. I had a table, a chair, I could read, write and smoke. I wrote to the commander two or three times, asking for the reason of my detention. I never received a reply.'

Hodys told Morgen that one night in December 1942, at 11 pm, an unexpected visitor turned up in her cell. It was camp commander Höss; he had sneaked into the building unnoticed, through his garden. He told her she had nothing to fear and asked why 'she always was so aloof towards him. I told him to me he was a respectable personality as commander and that he was married. … He asked me to be friends. Then he tried to kiss me again … . Again I urged him to go. Eventually, he went away and told me I had to think about it and that he would return.'

Two days later he visited her once again in her cell where they 'had a lengthy conversation lasting two hours about personal issues'. He was getting aggressive again. Hodys urged him to stop as the door to the cell was wide open and someone could see them. Höss left 'in a bad mood' and the next day he had her transferred to a cell that could be locked from the inside as well. When he secretly entered her cell again a few days later, he refused to leave, got into bed with her and forced her to have intercourse. Hodys claimed that later on she had been forced to have sex with the camp commander more often. One time, they were almost caught red-handed by a guard who was checking the cells, when the fire alarm sounded and the light was turned on. Höss shoved his uniform under the bed and hid in a corner next to the door. According to Hodys, his nightly visits came to an end in February 1943 when she did not feel well, she thought she suffered from an attack of gallstones. A physician established however that she was eight weeks pregnant. That could not have been from anyone else but the camp commander. She was given pills to trigger an abortion, but after taking one she was in so much pain that she threw the rest away.

After the failed attempt at abortion, she was again transferred to another cell. Her privileged position came to an abrupt end: she ended up in a 'narrow, dark hole where only a little fresh air could come in. ... You could only stand in there or sit on your knees ... .' She thought she could feel a corpse in the dark. She claimed to have had no way to wash herself over a period of nine weeks and for the last seventeen days she was unable to go to the bathroom either, so she had to relieve herself in the cell. While previously the guards had avoided her, now she was harassed by them: buckets of water were thrown over her and she was scolded. Eventually she was released from the stand-up cell and transferred to a normal cell again. She attempted once again to induce an abortion, this time with a long needle and green soap. 'Using a mirror, I started to try with the result I lost a lot of blood and the spots became rather infected. The whole attempt was without any result.'

Hodys claimed she was released from the camp prison around 26 June 1943.[3] That was a few months before Morgen and his colleagues launched their investigation in Auschwitz that autumn. In his interview with *The World at War*, Morgen declared however that it had been he who had liberated Hodys from her nasty position. He stated that he found her 'in a stand-up cell, a contraption in the basement made of concrete which was so small you only could get in by ducking deeply. The woman had been standing in there for weeks, naked with hardly anything to eat, except for the small amount that prisoners, who pitied her, managed to smuggle in. I came just in time to save her. Immediately, I took her out of the concentration camp and subsequently brought her to a Roman-Catholic hospital near Munich.'

According to him, Höss had intended to kill her so nobody would find out he had made her pregnant. 'The fear this woman felt for Höss was indescribable,' he stated.[4] Morgen pretended to be her saviour, but Hodys' statement – taken by himself – tells a different story. Hodys claimed to have been transferred to a penal company in the camp after her release from the Bunker in June 1943. Later on, in the camp hospital, she had a successful abortion. She worked for three months as a surveyor and later in the camp kitchen. Pending her transfer to Munich – where she was to work in a hospital – she was admitted to the camp hospital again, this time with bronchitis. While recovering she was infected with typhoid and was almost taken away to the gas chamber, but that was prevented by an SS man she did not name.[5]

The Austrian Auschwitz survivor Hermann Langbein, author of *Menschen in Auschwitz*, a study published in 1980 of the life of prisoners and guards in Auschwitz, presents another explanation. In his opinion Hodys smuggled jewellery for camp commander Höss, and when it became known, he locked her up and wanted her to die. Not Morgen but his associate *SS-Hauptsturmführer* Gerhard Wiebeck would have liberated her subsequently from the Bunker. That would have been in the spring of 1944.[6] It is possible that Hodys mistook the date of her release during her interrogation and that it actually happened a year later. The certainty with which she remembered all other dates is implausible in any case in view of the fact that she suffered physically and mentally during her incarceration and probably lost all sense of time in her dark cell. If she really was a year off, it could well have been that Morgen and Wiebeck – or one of them – were responsible for her release. It is remarkable however that in the transcript of the interrogation the incorrect date has been included.

Günther Reinecke, chief of the *Oberste SS- und Polizeigericht*, confirmed during the Nuremberg trial that it had been the investigative committee that had managed to transfer Hodys from Auschwitz to Munich after the judges had guaranteed her life would be safe.[7] The assertion of both Morgen and Wiebeck that Höss had wanted Hodys to be murdered seems a little overstated. Höss could have opted to have her executed immediately, which frequently happened to other inmates of the Bunker. The fact that Höss was no longer in Auschwitz from the end of 1943 until the summer of 1944, but was staying in Berlin where he held an administrative function, sheds another light on the riddle. *SS-Obersturmbannführer* Arthur Liebehenschel replaced him as commander of the *Stammlager*. He imposed a regime a little less harsh than his predecessor and granted a pardon to the inmates of the Bunker. Under his rule, the notorious stand-up cells were also abolished. Thus it cannot be excluded that neither Morgen nor Wiebeck but the new commander had been responsible for Hodys' release from the Bunker. But this does not match the date Hodys mentioned for her release, as on 26 June 1943 Höss had not yet been replaced by Liebehenschel.

In Hodys' interrogation, conducted by Morgen, a subtle description is given of a meeting she had with Höss in the presence of Wiebeck after her release from the Bunker. Höss reportedly said to her she had behaved well and that she had been put in the cell for her own safety. He claimed not to know why she ended up in the stand-up cell.[8] The precise reason for her imprisonment and the situation regarding her release remain in the dark. That he had had a sexual relationship with her is certain as he confirmed this personally to Richard Sonnenfeldt, chief interpreter of the American prosecution during the Nuremberg trial.[9] It is also certain that Hodys was staying in a hospital in Munich in the autumn of 1944 where she was interrogated by Morgen. Her period of imprisonment had not yet ended though, as from 12 March to 12 April 1945 she was registered as a prisoner in the police prison in Leipzig. After the war she was employed by the International Refugee Organization. In 1949 she flew via the Berlin Air Lift to Basle and subsequently she took residence in Italy. Ultimately, she emigrated to Canada.[10]

Chapter XIX

Thwarted in Auschwitz

The man who kicked off the Hodys issue, Morgen's informer *SS-Hauptscharführer* Gerhard Palitzsch, did not survive the war. There are rumours that he 'disappeared'. According to Heinz Höhne, the SS man 'who by order of Morgen collected evidence against camp commander Höss' disappeared in a penal bunker.[1] Raul Hilberg wrote: '*SS-Hauptscharführer* Palitzsch was discovered in Auschwitz in the presence of a Jewish woman and dumped into a coal bunker.'[2] Both investigators suggest Palitzsch was disposed of, probably by Höss or his cronies, in order to thwart Morgen's investigation. No irrefutable evidence exists, but it is not entirely unthinkable as Morgen's informer in Buchenwald, *SS-Hauptscharführer* Köhler, was also disposed of by colleagues who had poisoned him. Palitzsch however was not murdered, but arrested on suspicion of having had sexual relations with female inmates. Whether Morgen ordered his arrest is unclear. Palitzsch was released in November 1944; he was degraded to *SS-Schütze* – the lowest rank possible – and transferred to the *SS-Polizeipanzergrenadierdivision* of the *Waffen-SS*. It cannot be excluded that Palitzsch had been transferred by his superiors – for instance Oswald Pohl – to protect Höss or other high-ranking officers in Auschwitz. Palitzsch could not tell his story as he was killed in action in Hungary on 7 December 1944.[3]

The arrest and transfer of Palitzsch were not necessarily the result of a conspiracy against Morgen and his team of investigators. There is on the other hand a more solid indication justifying the conclusion that the investigation in Auschwitz was being thwarted. Both Morgen and his colleague Wilhelm Reimers reported that one night the wooden shed in which they had stored their evidence was destroyed by fire. 'The investigations in Auschwitz were interrupted and made difficult for a long time,' so Morgen said.[4] 'It was not possible to identify the executors of the obvious arson. Every member of the SS kept silent.' Remarkably, one of his associates was named as possible arsonist. According to camp guard

SS-Oberscharführer Wilhelm Claussen, rumours were circulating to the effect that SS judge Wilhelm Reimers started the fire. Reimers himself would have been suspected of theft from 'Canada' and had intended to destroy the evidence. Reimers denied the charge and argued he had fallen out of favour because of his rigorous investigation.[5] Because of the arrests he had ordered in Auschwitz, he was not popular among the camp staff and somebody had wanted to incriminate him. If Reimers was speaking the truth, there was question of a well-orchestrated obstruction of the investigation: not only all the evidence had been successfully destroyed, an attempt was also made to incriminate a member of the committee. Proof of this suspicion is not available.

During the Auschwitz trial in Frankfurt, Morgen voiced his assertion that the arson was part of a conspiracy, hatched at the top with Oswald Pohl as the sinister mastermind behind it. He argued Pohl did not only back up his corrupt personnel in the concentration camps but was corrupt himself as well. Along with his closest associates, he would have gold from the camps melted down and the equivalent deposited in an account. That way he could stash away hundreds of thousands of *Reichsmark*. In close cooperation with Heinrich Müller and Ernst Kaltenbrunner, Pohl tried, so Morgen claimed, 'every conceivable means of stopping me, gently at first and then with offers of a fabulous career in another section of the SS, then through typical military measures, through complaints to the *Reichsführer-SS* and the *Reichskriminalpolizei*, through massive threats, and finally through an attack on my investigative commission, in which our entire offices, barracks and files were destroyed through arson.'[6]

Holocaust researcher Raul Hilberg backed Morgen's declaration at least partially. In his opinion it was the 'almighty Pohl who shielded his commanders at the critical moment and supported them'.[7] According to Heinz Höhne, Pohl and his companions got what they wanted in April 1944. He wrote that Himmler ordered Morgen in mid-April to 'limit himself to the Koch case and suspend all other investigations'. He stated further, it was no coincidence that Himmler called a halt to Morgen's investigation just at the time his research focused on Auschwitz commander Höss. After all, Höss was 'the personification of hygienic mass murder ..., the ideal SS man Himmler believed in so strongly'.[8] But Höhne does not explain how it could be that in the autumn of 1944 Morgen interrogated Eleonore Hodys to gather evidence against Höss.

The testimony, delivered by former chief judge Günther Reinecke during the Nuremberg trial, offers more clarity. He testified that Himmler had indeed given the order in mid-April to the effect that 'the measures against Koch should mark the end of all criminal investigations in the concentration camps'. Himmler expected of the other culprits that they would voluntarily report their own crimes in the future, after which he might grant amnesty. Those who did not do so would be sentenced to death. Reinecke did not make it clear how crimes of camp staff could be tracked down when the investigative committee was disbanded, but he said it would not get that far. As Franz Breithaupt, chief of the *Hauptamt SS-Gericht*, who had protested against the order, had never received a definitive decision from Himmler, he assumed the *Reichsführer-SS* (RFSS) would tolerate future cases as well. Reinecke stated: 'The *Hauptamt SS-Gericht* at that time intentionally delayed the completion of the case against Koch so as to have an opportunity of extending the investigating activities to other camps, and that was actually achieved. The investigating commissions of the *Reichskriminalpolizei*, which had already been withdrawn as a result of Himmler's order, resumed their activities, and from the autumn of 1944 the investigations were continued on a broad scale. Authoritative powers, which were necessary in view of Pohl's lasting resistance, were issued by the special judge of the *Reichsführer* [possibly Hans Bender] and could not be ignored, not even by Pohl.'[9]

Morgen's personnel file also contains correspondence from which can be concluded he was still authorized to deal with cases other than Koch's after April 1944. It contains a letter from Franz Breithaupt, sent on 3 August 1944 to Hans Bender, the highest SS and Police Judge and member of the staff of the RFSS. In it Breithaupt remarks that Morgen had been seconded by Himmler to the *Reichskriminalpolizeiamt*, part of the RSHA, in the spring of 1943. Breithaupt no longer found it expedient for Morgen to remain in the *Reichskriminalpolizeiamt*. He protested against Morgen being answerable not only to the *Gerichtsherren* – the RFSS and himself – but simultaneously to the chiefs of the RSHA and the *Reichskriminalpolizeiamt*. 'This situation is untenable,' he stated, and asked Himmler to put an end to this situation by formally appointing Morgen investigative judge on the *SS-Gericht zur besonderen Verwendung* (Special SS court) of the *Hauptamt SS-Gericht*.

Bender's reply was sent on 26 August from Himmler's field headquarters. He confirmed he had submitted Breithaupt's letter to Himmler. The latter had ordered Morgen's secondment by the RSHA be lifted 'effective as of today' and to have him added as an investigative judge to the *zbv Gericht* (court for special purposes). The same day, Bender sent a message to Ernst Kaltenbrunner, chief of the RSHA, to inform him about the transfer of Morgen. The next decision by Himmler from the letter is important: he ordered that the transfer did not alter in any way Morgen's leadership of the investigative commissions established in the camps. In the letter even Himmler's appreciation was conveyed for the 'good work' Morgen had done in the concentration camps. Morgen was sent on a three-week leave during which he was not allowed to handle 'judicial matters'. Furthermore, Himmler ordered the promotion of Morgen and Bender to discuss with Morgen at a later date 'principal issues concerning to the leading of the investigation'. If and when this discussion took place is unknown but Morgen's promotion followed on 9 November 1944.[10]

So, April 1944 was not the end of Morgen's investigations in the concentration camps. The research in Auschwitz concentration camp was suspended though. Possibly Höhne's assumption is correct that this suspension was caused by the fact that Himmler wanted to prevent Höss from being arrested. Whatever it may be, it is remarkable that Höss was transferred to Berlin in November 1943, shortly after Morgen and his team had arrived in Auschwitz. In Berlin he was given a desk job as chief of a department within *Amtsgruppe D* of the SS-WVHA, the office that managed the concentration camps.[11] It is not unthinkable that the transfer had been arranged by Pohl or Himmler to prevent Morgen launching an investigation in Auschwitz against the camp commander. There is however no corroborative evidence for this and what we do know about the transfer points in two other directions. In the first place, the transfer seems to have been of an organizational nature: Pohl had decided that the three sections of Auschwitz – the *Stammlager*, Monowitz and Birkenau – would from then on be considered as separate camps, each with its own commander.[12] Consequently, the role of Höss as overall commander was over. In the second place, the transfer may probably have been of a personal nature: it is very likely that Höss was granted some rest with a desk function. In a post-war discussion with prison psychologist Leon Goldensohn, Höss told him that in his last year in Auschwitz he suffered

onrad Morgen as *SS-Untersturmführer*. (*Fritz auer Institut*)

SS chief Heinrich Himmler (left) with SA leader Ernst Röhm, August 1933. Röhm was killed on the orders of Hitler on 2 July 1934. (*Bundesarchiv, Bild 102-14886/CC-BY-SA*)

S-Standartenführer Hermann Fegelein. *Bundesarchiv, Bild 101III-Bueschel-056-13/ üschel/CC-BY-SA 3*)

SS-Oberführer Oskar Dirlewanger in 1944. (*Bundesarchiv, Bild 183-S73495/Anton Ahrens/ CC-BY-SA 3.0*)

Second from left is Konrad Morgen. Location, date and identity of the other persons are unknown (*Fritz Bauer Institut*)

Karl Otto Koch, camp commander of Buchenwald. (*Nuremberg Trials Archive, Harvard Law School Library/edited by Kaj Metz*)

...s and police officials speaking among themselves during a roll call of Polish prisoners in concentration ...mp Buchenwald. Karl Otto Koch is second from the left. (*United States Holocaust Memorial Museum,* *...urtesy of Robert A. Schmuhl*)

...oncentration camp Buchenwald, circa 1940. Newly arrived Polish prisoners undressing before they ...re washed and shaved. (*United States Holocaust Memorial Museum, courtesy of Robert A. Schmuhl*)

Prisoners from the Buchenwald concentration camp at forced labour building the Weimar-Buchenwald railway line. (*United States Holocaust Memorial Museum, courtesy of Gedenkstaette Buchenwald*)

Display on a table in liberated Buchenwald: Pieces of tattooed human skin, human body parts in spir and a lamp shade, probably made of human skin. (*US National Archives Washington/Public Domain*)

May 1945. A crate full of (wedding) rings confiscated from prisoners in Buchenwald. They were found by American troops in a cave near the camp, besides other valuables. The gold rings were to be melted and presented to the German National Bank. 'Every wedding ring here represents a home broken and a human murdered by the Germans,' according to the original caption. (*United States Holocaust Memorial Museum, courtesy of National Archives and Records Administration, College Park*)

Reconstruction of cell 115 in the Camp Vught National Memorial with on the wall the names of the women who died here during the Bunker tragedy. (*Jeroen Koppes/TracesOfWar.com*)

Odilo Globocnik (right), *SS- und Polizeiführer* Lublin and leader of *Aktion Reinhard*. This photo w taken in 1940. (*Bundesarchiv, Bild 146-1990-087-10/Unknown author/CC-BY-SA 3.0*)

Polish Jews from the ghetto of Siedlice are deported to Treblinka extermination camp in 1942. The extermination of the Jews from Poland was called Action Reinhard. (*Wikimedia Commons/ Public Domain*)

Prisoners in the section called 'Canada' unload a truck with clothing confiscated from new arrivals in Auschwitz-Birkenau, about May 1944. All confiscated items had to be sorted. Valuables had to be transferred to the Reich but were often embezzled by SS personnel. (*Yad Vashem/Public domain*)

Former Auschwitz commander Rudolph Höss (second from left) relaxing with other SS men at the Solahütte. The others are, from left to right: Joseph Mengele, Joseph Kramer and Anton Thumann. (*United States Holocaust Memorial Museum, courtesy of anonymous donor*)

SS officers and female auxiliaries (*Helferinnen*) having fun during their stay at the Solahütte, July 1944. Original caption translated in English: 'Suddenly, it started to rain.' (*United States Holocaust Memoria Museum, courtesy of Anonymous Donor*)

Wilhelm Boger. (*Landesgericht Frankfurt am Main*)

Maximilian Grabner. (*Auschwitz–Birkenau Museum*)

Ise Koch listens as her life sentence is read to her in Dachau, 15 August 1947. (*US National Archives Washington/Public domain*)

The reconstructed 'black wall' between the Blocks 10 and 11 in Auschwitz I concentration camp. Thousands of prisoners were executed here by shooting, both 'legally' and 'illegally'. (*Richard Broekhuijzen/ CC BY-SA 4.0*)

Rudolf Höss shortly before being hanged. (*Stanisław Dąbrowiecki/Wikimedia Commons/Public domain*)

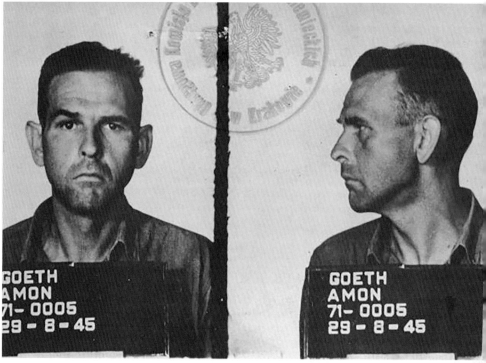

Mugshot of Amon Göth after his arrest by the Allies. He was the former commander of the Płaszów concentration camp. Date: 29 August 1945. (*Wikimedia Commons/Public Domain*)

Göth's villa at Płaszów. According to witnesses, he fired at prisoners from the balcony. (*John Smeets/TracesOfWar.com*)

A closer look at the balcony of Göth's villa. (*John Smeets/TracesOfWar.com*)

Dachau, 16 July 1946. Civilians and US Army military police wait outside the building where the Malmedy massacre trial is taking place. (*United States Holocaust Memorial Museum, courtesy of National Archives and Records Administration, College Park*)

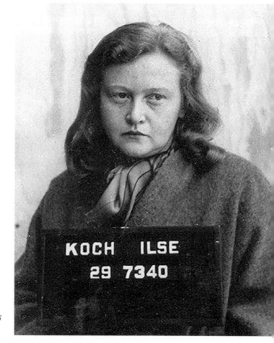

Ilse Koch after her arrest by the Americans. (*US National Archives Washington/Public domain*)

Konrad Morgen (sitting on the chair on the small stage) as a witness during an American trial against Nazi suspects in Dachau, 10 June 1947. (*US National Archives Washington/Public domain*)

The Nuremberg Palace of Justice, location of the post-war trials against the Nazi leadership. (*Henny van Loenen/TracesOfWar.com*)

Konrad Morgen on the witness stand in Nuremberg. (*US National Archives Washington/Public domain*)

In Camp Ohrdruf, Eisenhower and generals Patton and Bradley look at a funeral pyre with partially cremated corpses, 12 April 1945. (*Colonel Meches/US National Archives Washington/Public domain*)

American troops at the gateway of Buchenwald, 18 April, 1945. The concentration camp was liberated on 11 April 1945. (*Ardean R. Miller, US Signal Corps/National Archives, Washington*)

Citizens of Weimar are confronted by the Americans with the corpses of prisoners from Buchenwald, 16 April 1945. (*Walter Chichersky, US Signal Corps/National Archives, Washington*)

Oswald Pohl (standing) during his trial in Nuremberg in 1947. (*US National Archives Washington/Publ* *domain*)

Arrested Jewish women on a street in Budapest, October 1944. Konrad Morgen travelled to Budapest to investigate Adolf Eichmann, the SS-officer who managed the Final Solution. (*Bundesarchiv, Bil* *101I-680-8285A-08/Faupel/CC-BY-SA 3.0*)

from tensions: 'I felt exhausted, not only because of the gassings but also because the other work. My wife complained about my not being with my family more often and that I was married to my job. As late as 1943, when I went to Berlin, my doctors reported to my superiors I was over-fatigued and exhausted.' While his wife and children – his wife was pregnant with their last child – had remained in Auschwitz, towards the end of 1943 he took a six-week holiday in the mountains all by himself.[13]

On 8 May 1944, Höss temporarily returned to Auschwitz, not as camp commander but to supervise the extermination of the Hungarian Jews that was carried out in Auschwitz-Birkenau in the spring and summer of 1944.[14] This massive extermination project was pointedly called *Aktion Höss*. Only one month previously, Himmler had suspended Morgen's investigation in the camp. It may well be that he had the investigation suspended to prevent Morgen and his team getting in the way of the extermination. The 'processing' of almost 400,000 Jews in a period of just eight weeks was the biggest challenge ever faced by the personnel in Auschwitz; a gruesome project of prestige. The camp staff had to focus itself entirely on the task allotted to it and did not want to be hindered by Morgen and his colleagues who might have thwarted the progress of the operation by interrogating or arresting camp staff. Above all it was unthinkable that Höss – the extermination expert *par excellence* – would be prosecuted at exactly this important moment, certainly not for something as 'irrelevant' as a sexual relation with a female inmate. Lower-ranking functionaries like Maximilian Grabner and the thoroughly corrupt Karl Koch could be sacrificed to keep up a veil of justice, but the arrest and conviction of a prominent executor of the *Endlösung* like Höss would at that time constitute too big a threat to the progress of this extermination project in Auschwitz.

On 29 June 1944 Höss returned to Berlin and in the autumn of 1944 a belated investigation into him was launched, occasioned by the incriminating testimony Eleonore Hodys had presented to Konrad Morgen in Munich. In Günther Reinecke's view the investigation focused on the suspicion that Höss had been involved in the 'murder of an unknown number of persons' in Auschwitz. It probably pertained to 'illegal' murders that had taken place in the Bunker and had been witnessed by Hodys during the period she had been imprisoned there herself. During the Nuremberg trial however, Reinecke stressed that 'proceedings against

Höss had not advanced sufficiently to serve an indictment against him. It was still in the process of preliminary investigation. Material had to be collected first.'[15] In the case against Höss, Morgen never got beyond this phase, which was mainly due to the disastrous progress of the war for Germany.

After the German defeat at Stalingrad in February 1943, the situation deteriorated fast at the German front. The Red Army had pulled itself together and managed to turn the tide with an overwhelming military force. As the Soviet juggernaut advanced on Germany, the western Allies landed in Normandy on 6 June 1944 to begin the liberation of western Europe. In the east the first concentration camps fell into enemy hands. Due to the approaching Red Army, Majdanek concentration camp was evacuated in July 1944 and was liberated on 24 July. In Auschwitz the gas chambers were closed down after members of the Jewish *Sonderkommando* had revolted and had blown up one of the crematory buildings on 7 October. To erase the traces of their crimes, the SS had destroyed the remaining buildings afterwards. Incriminating documents from the camp administration were burned. The camp was closed on 18 January 1945 after most of the remaining 58,000 inmates had been evacuated to the west. On 27 January the first Soviet soldiers entered the camp, where they encountered 7,650 inmates. Most were so weakened they died after their liberation.[16] In the same period, German cities were subjected to continuous Allied bombardments. Inhabitants of Berlin and other cities had to survive somehow among the rubble, in expectation of what would happen to them once the vengeful soldiers of the Red Army invaded their country.

Conditions were far from ideal for Morgen and his team to continue their case against Höss, if only due to the developments at the front, as they were no longer able to travel to Auschwitz to search for evidence. At the end of 1944 Morgen could not count on support from the SS leadership any longer in his attempts to prosecute Höss. With the Red Army advancing on Berlin and committing numerous atrocities on the way, it is hardly likely that anyone would be bothered about a camp commander who had possibly violated the rules. Höss was never to appear before an SS judge. Indeed it is questionable if he would have done so even if conditions had been more favourable for Morgen. The former camp commander was on good terms with Himmler and an old friend of Martin Bormann, Hitler's powerful secretary. Both men could have stopped the prosecution of Höss effortlessly. Someone with such powerful patrons and an excellent service record had nothing to fear from Morgen and his investigative committee. At the end of the day, it was a Polish court that sentenced Höss to death after the war; on 16 April 1947 he was hanged in Auschwitz.

Chapter XX

The Hell of Płaszów

The last known investigation in the concentration camps Morgen and his team occupied themselves with was into the notorious camp commander *SS-Hauptsturmführer* Amon Göth, who became known above all from the movie *Schindler's List* of 1993 in which he was impersonated by actor Ralph Fiennes.

Göth, born in Vienna on 11 December 1908, the son of a successful publisher, had enrolled in the juvenile branch of the Austrian NSDAP at the age of seventeen. The party advocated unification between Germany and Austria, and in order to achieve that goal, violence was not shunned. Consequently, the party was prohibited in 1933 and the Austrian authorities started a manhunt against Nazis suspected of crimes against the state and society. Göth fled to Germany that year to evade prosecution. From Germany he and other National Socialist exiles continued the campaign of terror against the Austrian state. He smuggled radio equipment into his native country where it was used to spread propaganda and he worked as a courier for the SS. After having been *Bewerber* of the SS since 1930, he became a fully-fledged member in 1932. October 1933 saw Göth arrested by the Austrian police but he was released during the Christmas holidays for lack of evidence. Subsequently he was involved in the failed putsch by the Austrian Nazi party on 25 July 1934, which claimed the life of the Christian-Socialist Engelbert Dollfuß.

In March 1938 Austria was incorporated into the *Reich* under German pressure. Probably due to a conflict with a superior, Göth was expelled from the SS in 1934, but following the *Anschluss* he was reinstated. At the outbreak of war he joined the SS full time. After having held administrative functions, he was transferred to Lublin in 1942 as member of the staff of *SS- und Polizeiführer* Odilo Globocnik who was in charge of *Aktion Reinhard*.[1] Subsequently, from 11 February to 13 September 1944 he was commander of the Płaszów labour camp, located in a Krakow suburb.

The camp opened in the summer of 1942 and was partially built on top of two Jewish cemeteries. It housed 12,000 inmates in the second half of 1943. After it had become a concentration camp in January 1944, the number of inmates rose to 24,000 in June 1944.[2] The prisoners, mostly Jews, were deployed in factories and workshops in and around the camp and in the nearby stone quarry under inhuman conditions.

Apart from his function as camp commander, Göth was also actively involved in dismantling ghettos and labour camps for Jews in the vicinity of Krakow in the same period. Various witnesses have confirmed that in the process Göth displayed extreme violence and derived great pleasure from executing victims himself. During the dismantlement of the ghetto in Tarnów – a city some 43 miles east of Krakow – on 3 September 1943 he allegedly killed between thirty and ninety women and children himself.[3] Previously, the evacuation of the ghetto of Krakow – 13 and 14 March 1943 – had degenerated into a bloodbath. Four thousand Jews, including hospital patients, children and elderly, were murdered on the spot by Göth and his men. The remaining ghetto inhabitants were transferred to Auschwitz and Płaszów where many of them died.[4]

Göth is most notorious for the reign of terror he imposed in Płaszów camp. To humiliate his Jewish prisoners, he had the road to the camp paved with the tombstones of the Jewish cemeteries. But he was not limited to pestering alone; various inmates testified after the war to the bloodlust of the feared camp commander. 'One day, Göth was not satisfied with the work we performed in the various workshops,' former prisoner Taube Biber recalls. 'He was a bloodthirsty monster and he yelled: *Appell!* We stood in rows of five. … As Göth walked by, he selected 25 girls and they were whiplashed 25 times on their backs. When it was all over and we went back to the barracks we saw that the girls had been beaten black and blue and blood was running down their backs.' Another former prisoner, Joseph Perl, declared: 'Amon Göth was a sadist. He had a small balcony and he derived his greatest pleasure from shooting people from there. If he had not shot some 30 people before breakfast, it tasted bad. He never spoke to inmates, he just shot them.'[5]

After the war, a Polish court held Göth responsible for the death of 8,000 inmates in camp Płaszów.[6] Apart from his sadism, Göth was known for his exorbitant life style which was characterized by parties involving much alcohol and many women that he paid for with black-marketeering and plunder. He enriched himself by using valuables he had confiscated from Jews when the ghetto in Krakow was dismantled and which he should have transferred to the *Reichsbank*.[7] It included gold, savings, clothing and furniture. After the war a Polish court valued the stolen goods and in particular the valuable possessions at many millions of zlotys, according to the rate of exchange at the time.[8] He served food, actually meant for his undernourished inmates, at his parties or sold it on the black market. These illegal practices could not remain unnoticed, and on 13 September 1944 Göth was arrested by the SS on charges of suspicion of corruption, maltreatment and murder.[9] Morgen's associates probably conducted the investigation, although he indicated at the Nuremberg trial he had also visited Płaszów camp personally.[10]

How Morgen and his team found out about Göth's crimes is not known for certain. A possible cause was a letter to Heinrich Himmler, written by Hans Stauber, the highest financial official of the German garrison in Krakow. In his letter, dated 16 August 1944, Stauber voiced his concern about the loss of Jewish labourers as a result of the evacuation of Płaszów. Because of the advancing Red Army that summer, the camp management had started to evacuate the camp – it would be liberated in January 1945. Inmates were evacuated to Auschwitz and other concentration camps located further to the west; many of them perished before reaching their final destination. The only reason Jewish inmates were still alive at that moment was that they provided forced labour for the *Wehrmacht* in the armaments industry, which suffered from a serious shortage of workers at this stage of the war. Stauber urged Himmler to see to it that 'at this moment, everybody should deploy himself to the best of his ability and all efforts be directed at that single great goal, the imminent final victory'. Moreover, he complained about the management of the camp. He claimed cigarettes were taken away from prisoners to be distributed among guards. They would also have inmates pay high prices for bread which might previously have been stolen from other inmates. All of this, according to Stauber, 'threw a harsh light on the lack of supervision in the camp'.[11]

Another cause for the discovery of Göth's crimes was suggested by Mietek Pemper, an inmate who worked in Göth's office. He said dissatisfied SS men had lodged complaints about their commander. They thought he treated them cruelly and were indignant about the fact that he had brought charges against them with the *SS- und Polizeigericht*. For instance, Göth is supposed to have brought charges against an SS man for stealing a small amount of money. The SS man would have told the court he could not understand why he had been punished so severely while 'the commander possessed a fortune of valuable items and foreign currencies'. Another explanation comes from Oskar Schindler, the German industrialist who employed Jewish inmates from Płaszów in his enamel factory. Thanks to him, many of his employees survived the war. In 1946 Schindler declared that indignation had emerged within the SS because Göth had two Jewish inmates executed because he believed they were spies for Himmler.[12] Not a very plausible explanation and further evidence does not exist.

Whatever the occasion for Morgen's investigative commission may have been, after Göth's arrest the camp was freed of its tyrannical commander. According to Mietek Pemper, it seemed like 'the Pope had been arrested for stealing gold spoons'.[13] During the six-month investigation, numerous witnesses were interrogated, including Oskar Schindler. As he was suspected of having bribed Göth, he was arrested as well. According to the factory owner, Göth had attempted to put the blame on him by claiming that the 80,000 RM found in the villa of the camp commander had originated from him. Göth would also have stated that all contraband found in the camp belonged to Schindler. Schindler denied all charges, and in consequence of his good relations with high-ranking persons within the *Wehrmacht* he was released after a little more than a week from the *Gestapo* prison in Krakow.[14] The charges against Schindler were not entirely unjustified: by bribing high-ranking officials including Göth and buying food on the black market, he managed to save over a thousand Jews for which, after the war, he was awarded the title Righteous among the Nations by Yad Vashem, the Israeli Holocaust Institute.

Mietek Pemper also testified against Göth in the case against him that was opened by the SS. As clerk of Płaszów camp he could provide the SS research team with valuable information on Göth's clandestine activities. He told his interrogators how the camp commander had expropriated camp food and the personal possessions of the Jews. Pemper declared after the war that one of Morgen's associates had spoken out against Göth's cruel treatment of inmates. In the stone quarry near the camp the commander had the habit of tying women to a small train with a wagon loaded with nine tons of stones. The heavy load had to be pulled up the steep incline by the women between twelve and fifteen times. This destructive labour was called the *Mannschaftszug*. Morgen's colleague said that this kind of work was 'equal to a death sentence' for prisoners – it entailed 'extremely hard work combined with beatings and often leading to death'. Pemper claimed that Morgen's people had further discovered that Göth had various inmates killed because they knew too much about his crimes. The SS research team also charged Göth with having granted inmates access to 'secret documents and other papers that prisoners were not allowed to see' including assessments of camp guards, only to be read by officers.[15]

Despite the incriminating evidence the research team had collected, Göth was released on personal bail from the prison in Breslau on 22 October 1944. Early in 1945 the case against him was reopened but without success: he was to remain a free man until the end of the war.[16] In the spring of 1945 he even paid an unexpected visit to Oskar Schindler, whose factory had meanwhile been relocated to Brněnec – Brünnlitz in German – in Czechia. He came to inspect his property Schindler had stored for him in exchange for a few trucks the entrepreneur had needed to move machines and other items to his new plant. Among Göth's possessions were furniture from his villa, 200,000 Polish cigarettes, jewellery and other valuables.[17] Eventually, Amon Göth was arrested by American troops in February 1945, while he was staying in an SS sanatorium in Bad Tolz. He was imprisoned in the former concentration camp at Dachau and subsequently turned over to the Polish authorities. A Polish tribunal in Krakow sentenced him to death and he was hanged in Krakow on 13 September 1946. Before he was hanged, he allegedly gave the Hitler salute.[18]

Chapter XXI

An Unexpected Defeat

Little is known about Konrad Morgen's activities after New Year 1945, but his investigation in concentration camps seems to have ground to a halt. In this period the concentration camps in Germany were flooded with inmates, evacuated from camps in the east of the crumbling *Reich*. The camps in the west became overcrowded and as a result of malnutrition and the outbreak of epidemics, inmates died in huge numbers. In the increasing chaos it was senseless for Morgen to continue his investigations in the camps. In the autumn of 1944 he had been appointed SS chief judge in Krakow. He occupied himself only with routine judicial issues and felt he had been sidetracked.[1] He probably left Krakow around 17 January 1945 when the seat of the General Government in Krakow was lifted and the German administration evacuated. The Red Army captured the city on 19 January 1945. Morgen was transferred to Breslau, today Wrocław in Poland. After the Red Army had laid siege to the city on 13 February, the German garrison surrendered on 6 May.

After the war, Morgen said that after what he had seen in Auschwitz 'I could only shiver when I thought of Germany's future. I said to myself, "once we have lost this war, our enemies will tear us to pieces".' Despite Germany's catastrophic situation, Morgen argued he had not seen the defeat coming. He expected Hitler to have a last trump card up his sleeve and he would succeed again, just like he had succeeded with the Autobahn and the invasions of Poland and France. Only at the last moment did Morgen change his view.[2] It is remarkable that, even in the last stages of the Third Reich, in a letter to his future wife, Maria Wachter, he spoke highly of Heinrich Himmler despite all the crimes committed in his name that he had witnessed. In January he wrote to her how a speech by the *Reichsführer-SS*, delivered in the previous summer, had boosted the morale of himself and his colleagues: 'The speech is still having a tremendous effect on us today, and has influenced me and everyone deeply. He spoke of the virtues of an officer. From that, one realized how un-German we have become. The speech was delivered with an openness not previously seen. The RFSS showed himself a great man with a sensitive heart, unexpectedly practical in matters concerning the troops.'[3]

Even after the failed Ardennes offensive in the winter of 1944/5, Hitler's troops continued fighting. Many Germans fostered hope that Hitler's wonder weapons – the V-1 flying bomb and the V-2 rocket – would still lead Germany to victory. In March 1945 the Allies crossed the Rhine and advanced further into Germany. The Red Army had captured Warsaw in January 1945, and in April 1945 the battle for the German capital was unleashed. It ended on 2 May in victory for the Red Army. A few days later, on 8 May, the Germans accepted unconditional surrender on all fronts. More than a week before, on 30 April, Hitler had committed suicide in his subterranean bunker in Berlin. Morgen stated after the war he was glad that Hitler had not been killed but had committed suicide, ample proof of his failure. Should he have died in an attempt at murder, there would be, according to Morgen, 'still National Socialists today who would say that if he had not been murdered, he would have succeeded'.[4] In hindsight, Morgen thought fighting to the last senseless. He wondered how people at the top could have continued the battle so that 'even the last remains of Germany would be destroyed? No government can be that criminal.'[5]

For a short while Morgen was a prisoner of war of the Soviets and the Czechs but soon became a free man again. How he was released is unknown. He probably managed to hide from the Russians and the Czechs that he had held a high rank in the SS. While many former SS men went into hiding or attempted to escape from Europe in fear of being prosecuted, Morgen reported to the western Allies of his own accord after he had learned he was wanted because of his 'knowledge of concentration camps'.[6] On 22 September 1945 he left Prien in Bavaria and arrived at the headquarters of the American Counter Intelligence Corps of the 7th Army in the Seckenheim suburb of Mannheim.[7] He showed himself willing to testify about the crimes he had investigated during the war. Major Paul Kubala, commander of the 7th Army Interrogation Center, noted that Morgen had discovered much corruption up to the highest ranks of the SS and that he possessed a vast knowledge of the activities of the SS in Poland during the occupation. Regarding his experience as an investigator, so concluded Kubala, he seemed able to provide a detailed description of numerous war crimes.[8] That was the beginning of Morgen's role as a witness in various trials against war criminals that were held in subsequent years. Apart from being a witness himself, due to his position within the SS he was a defendant at the same time.

After having been transferred to CIC headquarters in Oberursel in Hessen for interrogation, defendant Morgen was moved to the former Dachau concentration camp which was being used at the time by the Americans as a prison camp for Germans suspected of war crimes. The camp had a capacity of 30,000 people. Over a period of three years various trials were held here, for instance against members of the staff of the Dachau, Mauthausen, Flossenbürg, Buchenwald, Mühldorf and Dora-Nordhausen camps. Members of *Kampfgruppe Peiper*, a unit of the *Waffen-SS*, also stood trial there on suspicion of murder of American PoWs during the Ardennes offensive. Staff members of the Hadamar euthanasia centre were indicted as well, as was *SS-Obersturmbannführer* Otto Skorzeny who had been in charge of German soldiers who had to infiltrate behind American lines during the Ardennes offensive wearing American uniforms. A total of 1,672 German suspects were subpoenaed by the American tribunal in Dachau. 1,416 of them were sentenced, 279 to life and 297 to death; in later years many prison terms were reduced and some of the death sentences were never carried out.[9]

Among the defendants in Dachau prison camp, there were a few who had previously been subjected to criminal investigation by Morgen. 'It so happened I was imprisoned along with the men I had indicted myself before.'[10] One of these was *SS-Hauptsturmführer* Hermann Hackmann who had been arrested by Morgen in Buchenwald concentration camp on suspicion of corruption. An SS court sentenced him to death but he beat the hangman by being placed in a penal unit. In Dachau, the Americans indicted him for the crimes he had committed in Buchenwald where he was employed prior to his transfer to Majdanek. The American military tribunal sentenced him to death, but again he dodged his penalty. He was granted amnesty in 1955 and released from the prison in Landsberg. Subsequently he was employed as salesman and agent in a furniture store until he was sentenced to ten years during the Majdanek trial on 30 June 1981 in Düsseldorf. He passed away in 1994.[11]

Chapter XXII

The Bitch of Buchenwald

Another person who was prosecuted by both the Americans in Dachau and by Konrad Morgen was Ilse Koch. Since the American tribunal in Dachau, her name is synonymous with the atrocities in the concentration camps. The blonde wife of the camp commander was accused of the most atrocious crimes and became notorious in Germany as *Die Hexe von Buchenwald*. In the American media, she became known as the Bitch of Buchenwald.

The former typist in a cigarette firm in Dresden was married in 1936 at the age of 30 to Karl Koch, ten years her senior. Together they moved to Buchenwald where he was appointed camp commander. Ilse benefitted from the huge sums of money her husband managed to embezzle. Inmates built a riding hall for her, valued at a quarter of a million RM.[1] Morgen noted in his report on the case in Buchenwald that 'Frau Koch possesses a character that with respect to greed, haughtiness and cruelty was no less than that of her husband'.[2] He called her a nymphomaniac and accused her of having had sexual relations with her husband's colleagues.

Within the camp she became notorious for her sadism. Morgen learned from witnesses that the commander's wife often provocatively strolled about the camp in 'a short skirt and see-through blouse'. She had male prisoners who dared to look at her punished by the sadistic camp guard Martin Sommer. Victims were usually subjected to twenty-five lashes with a stick; one of them is said to have succumbed to this flogging. She is said to have whipped inmates while riding her horse. Morgen had Ilse Koch arrested on 25 August 1943 on suspicion of complicity to the crimes of her husband, after which she spent seventeen months in preliminary custody in the police prison in Weimar until she was acquitted by an SS court. In June 1945 she was arrested by the American Army.

Ilse Koch became most notorious as a result of the accusation that she had had gloves, book covers and other utensils made from the skins of inmates she had selected herself. After the liberation of the camp the

Americans put all the items they had found on public display, among them preserved human organs, tattooed human skin, and a lamp with a shade allegedly made from human skin. The accusation that Ilse Koch had had this made formed the spearhead of the American tribunal in Dachau, but tangible evidence was lacking as it mysteriously disappeared.[3] A thorough search was conducted, carried out by Morgen himself, but it turned up nothing. To have irrefutable evidence available, the Americans in Dachau allegedly attempted to have Morgen sign a false declaration confirming that the accusation towards Ilse Koch regarding the lampshade was correct. As much as he detested the sadistic character of the camp commander's wife, Morgen refused to sign the declaration, despite being threatened, in his own words, to be transferred to the Russians after his first refusal, who would surely 'beat him to death'. He was 'severely beaten' – by his American captors – after his second and third refusal.[4] He claimed it was nothing compared to the way other prisoners were treated. He accused the Americans of having the 'small fish – Nazis who never had seen a concentration camp from less than a mile away – being flogged with chains. They were forced to drink gasoline and were put in stiflingly hot cells in order to force them to confess to crimes they had never committed.'[5]

Morgen's accusations towards the Americans were no coincidence. The intention of the Americans was to offer German war criminals a fair trial, but in reality proceedings did not always match the standards befitting a democratic constitutional state. The gruesome images of liberated concentration camps had led to severe international indignation, resulting in enormous public pressure to get as many defendants sentenced as possible. Sometimes methods were applied that would later be disqualified. It occurred for instance in the case against the 73 members of *Kampfgruppe Peiper* who were indicted for having caused the bloodbath of American prisoners of war at Baugnez near Malmédy during the Ardennes offensive. On 16 July 1946, 43 of them were sentenced to death and 22 to life imprisonment.[6] Influenced by the American home front that cried revenge for the slaughter in the Ardennes, the Americans allegedly forced the Germans to confess by using unacceptable means. Before the real thing, mock trials were held to put the defendants under pressure, they were allegedly beaten and deprived of drinking water for days, and some claimed they had to undergo 'fake hangings': a noose was tied around their neck and they were pulled up a few times until unconsciousness set in.[7]

The issue triggered widespread social indignation in Germany, but in America commotion emerged as well, in particular in states with a large number of inhabitants of German descent. Still relatively unknown Republican Senator Joseph McCarthy strongly fanned the flames in a tone comparable to that he would later use against the 'red danger'. He obviously wanted to gain political advantage regarding the large group of German-Americans living in his state.[8] Authorities could do nothing else but thoroughly investigate the case. An American Senate Committee presented its findings in October 1949, stating there was no plausible evidence for the charges pertaining to the physical maltreatment of the defendants. The committee did acknowledge however that the defendants had been put under mental pressure and not everything had proceeded correctly; the mock trials for instance were considered 'a grave mistake'.[9] As a result of the doubts that had arisen regarding the gathering of evidence and the public indignation triggered by it, the death sentences were not executed. Between 1948 and 1956 all the suspects were released from prison.[10] This amnesty must be seen against the background of the Cold War: in the meantime Western Germany had become an ally of the Americans in their struggle against Communism and leniency towards the German war criminals was deemed necessary so as not to compromise the good relations with the German Federal Republic.

The criminal prosecution of Ilse Koch proceeded in a no less whimsical way. On 14 August 1947 in Dachau she was sentenced to life. She was only spared the death sentence as she had become pregnant during her imprisonment (by a fellow prisoner or a prison guard). Ten witnesses were subpoenaed by the court, including a Franciscan monk who had been imprisoned in Buchenwald. He testified that one day he had seen Ilse Koch taking the number of an inmate with a conspicuous tattoo of a sailing ship. That same night, the inmate was summoned by the camp guards; then he disappeared forever. Six months later the monk claimed he saw, in pathology, a piece of prepared skin with the tattoo on it. Later he saw the tattoo again on the cover of a photo album belonging to Ilse Koch. The American prosecutor, however, was unable to present in evidence either this photo album or any other items made from human skin, because they, like the lampshade, had disappeared. Koch denied she had possessed such items and stated her position in the camp was being overestimated; she had just been a housewife and a mother.

On 8 June 1948 her life sentence was tacitly reduced to four years. When this became known in the United States, it triggered much commotion. People recalled how she had been portrayed during the trial as the personification of evil. How could anyone be punished so lightly? In the media bitter editorials appeared. 'Probably our army has revised the verdict only to enable Koch to start her lampshades plant again,' wrote *The New York Times*. The *New York Mirror* called for 'opening the cells in Atlanta, Leavenworth and Alcatraz where soldiers have to serve a 20 year sentence only because they had slapped an officer at some time'. At a trade fair of German industry in New York, hundreds of people protested, carrying slogans like: 'How much do Koch lamp shades cost?' And when the German boxer Hein ten Hoff came to America for a fight, the placards read: 'When will Ilse Koch come and fight?'[11]

General Lucius D. Clay, the military governor in the American zone of occupation in Germany, responsible for the reduction of Koch's sentence, defended himself by stating 'the reduction of her sentence was in accordance with the principles of American justice'. In his opinion the reduction was not an act of benevolence but a result of the study of judicial files. From those it transpired that the accusations against Koch were not based on hard evidence but on hearsay. The declarations of the witnesses turned out to be not entirely trustworthy. The witness mentioned above turned out not to be a Franciscan monk at all, but in reality someone who had offered – for a sizable reward – to testify against SS men. His testimony was contradictory as well: first he claimed to have seen the tattoo on Koch's photo album, but later it was a lampshade on which he had seen the tattoo. Two American correspondents who had been shown the album also testified that it could not have been made of human skin and that there was no tattoo on it.[12] There was hard evidence though that in Buchenwald human skin had been conserved. An American pathologist investigated three pieces of tattooed human skin found in Buchenwald and ascertained they were of human origin. According to Morgen, these tattooed pieces of skin were removed from the corpses of gypsies and criminals for criminal research. The existence of a lampshade made of human skin has never been established convincingly. The involvement of Ilse Koch in the preparation of human skin has never been proved either.[13]

'The power of propaganda and mass suggestion has never been illustrated better than in the case against Ilse Koch,' so the sharp conclusion read that was formulated in the revision report that was presented to General Clay. 'Long before the trial she had already been publicly condemned as the "bitch of Buchenwald". ... Stories about her went from mouth to mouth and were blown up with increasingly colourful details. But when it came down to presentation before a court, it turned out that evidence for these stories was lacking.'[14]

A Senate investigation committee ascertained nonetheless on 27 December 1948 that Koch had been involved in killing and maltreating hundreds of inmates. 'This bestial woman's guilt in specific murders is irrefutably established.'[15] Nevertheless Ilse Koch was released from American captivity on 17 October 1949, only to be taken into preliminary custody again by the German authorities. Under pressure from the enormous upheaval and the fact that the United States could not prosecute her again after she had served her sentence, Clay had urged the Germans to take her to a German court. Including her trial during the war, this was the third time she had stood trial for her crimes in Buchenwald.[16] She was indicted for murder and on 15 January 1951 was sentenced to life for the second time. She still protested her innocence. During her imprisonment psychiatrists diagnosed her as 'a pervert, a nymphomaniac and a hysteric, power hungry demon'. On 1 September 1967 she committed suicide in a Bavarian prison at the age of 61. 'I cannot do otherwise. Death is the only deliverance,' she wrote to her son, born in 1947 during her captivity.[17]

Chapter XXIII

Lies and Half-truths in Nuremberg

On 21 February 1945, the bell tower of the *Justizpalast* (Palace of Justice) in Nuremberg collapsed with loud noises and an enormous cloud of dust. That day, the building had taken five direct hits during an Allied aerial bombardment. The bronze statue of Lady Justitia on the bell tower landed among the rest of the rubble in the inner yard. The fall of the statue could have been symbolic of the demise of the constitutional state in Nazi Germany. Although other parts of the building were damaged as well, the building, in comparison to the neighbouring buildings, had survived relatively unscathed when the Americans captured the town on 20 April 1945. For seven months the American, British, French and Russian flags flew over the portico at the front of the building, grouped together fraternally. From 20 November 1945 until 1 October 1946 the International Military Tribunal was held in the building, led by the four major Allied powers. Apart from twenty-two high-ranking officials of the Nazi regime, six organizations stood trial as well: the NSDAP, SS, *Sicherheitsdienst* (SD), *Gestapo*, *Sturmabteilung* (SA) and the *Oberkommando der Wehrmacht* (OKW).

In Nuremberg, a role as witness for the defence had been reserved for Konrad Morgen, still in Allied captivity. On 7 and 8 August 1946 – the 197th and 198th day of the international tribunal – he underwent his baptism of fire when he was called as a witness by Dr Horst Pelckmann, counsel of the SS. The testimony he was about to deliver was diametrically opposed to everything that had become known meanwhile about the crimes of Himmler's 'elite corps'. The amount of evidence for the criminal nature of the SS had become overwhelming. In the courtroom, movies were shown of the horrific scenes which had been encountered during the liberation of the concentration camps. Various witnesses had testified about the crimes in the camps and the extermination of the Jews. Apart from former camp inmates, various culprits had been subpoenaed as witnesses, including Rudolph Höss, who gave a description of the extermination of the Jews in Auschwitz, and Otto Ohlendorf, who reported on the mass executions which had been carried out under his command by *Einsatzgruppe D* in the southern part of the Soviet Union. While the tribunal was flooded by the vast amount of incriminating evidence, Morgen's testimony was to polish up the image of the SS as a criminal organization. The intention of the defence was to present Morgen's investigations into maltreatment and illegal murders in the concentration camps as evidence that crimes were not permitted within the SS and were to be attributed to criminal individuals. Morgen's testimony would degenerate to a desperate attempt to rehabilitate the SS.

Counsel Pelckmann interrogated Morgen about his pre-war life. In his reply he stressed, probably afraid of being prosecuted himself for his membership of the SS, that he had been forcibly posted to the *Allgemeine-SS*. To present himself favourably, he also said he had written a book about war propaganda and the prevention of war. Subsequently he told that he had been appointed in 1943 to launch an investigation into corruption in Buchenwald and other concentration camps. The prosecutors listened in disbelief how he described the conditions in the camps. Counsel Pelckmann asked Morgen whether the impression was correct that the concentration camp were 'places for the extermination of human beings'. Morgen denied this and stated that his first visit to camp Buchenwald 'was a great surprise to me. The camp is situated on wooded heights, with a wonderful view. The installations were clean and freshly painted. There was much lawn and flowers. The prisoners were healthy, normally fed, sun-tanned, working.'

Morgen told the court that the new camp commander 'aimed at providing the prisoners with an existence worthy of human beings. They had regular mail service. They had a large camp library, even books in foreign languages. They had variety shows, motion pictures, sporting contests and even had a brothel.'[1] It was the ideal image of the concentration camps Morgen maintained in his post-war interview with American historian John Toland. He told Toland that an acquaintance had once asked him about an uncle in Buchenwald from whom nothing had been heard for a long time. Morgen promised to find out what had happened to the man. It turned out he was still imprisoned in Buchenwald where he had found work as a carpenter. When Morgen asked him if he would like to return to his family and offered to help him with it, the man turned down his help and allegedly said that he fared far better in the camp than at home. Morgen claimed that food for the concentration camp inmates was better than that for the German population and that they could buy as many cigarettes as they liked. Inmates were also allowed to receive Red Cross parcels regularly. He also referred to a quip about Richard Glücks, the inspector of the concentration camps. When Glücks was out of coffee one day during the war, he went to camp Sachsenhausen where this scarce commodity was offered to him by a prisoner.[2]

To Pelckmann's question whether it was possible he had been misled during his visits to the concentration camps, as had been the case with the Jews in the extermination camps, Morgen answered: 'I was not just a visitor of a concentration camp, but I took residence there for a long time. I can almost say I lived there. It is almost impossible to be misled for such a long time. … I do not want to say that I, despite these strenuous efforts, was unable to be informed about all crimes but I believe there was no question of misleading in regard to what I experienced.' Pelckmann concluded that Morgen described the concentration camps as 'extremely pleasant'. When he asked him if he could name any negative points, Morgen replied: 'I did not want to say that concentration camps were sanatoria or a paradise for the inmates. If they had been, my investigation would have been useless.' Morgen said that he, through his work, 'gained an insight into the extremely dark and sinister side of the concentration camps'. He stated that inmates in practice had no rights whatsoever. 'Once inside the camp, it was almost impossible to get out.' An inmate had to 'fear that each moment, crimes could be committed against him'. All the same, Morgen did not have the impression the camp management had the intention to 'create a criminal system but inevitably, individual crimes had to occur as a result of these conditions.'

These individual crimes committed by camp guards were nonetheless toned down by Morgen. In his opinion, criminal prosecution remained limited to between 0.5 and 3 per cent of the total camp staff and that was 'the usual army rate'. He also remarked that some camp commanders he met did everything humanly possible for their prisoners. 'I met doctors whose every effort it was to help sick prisoners and to prevent further sickness.' In his opinion, prisoners were accomplices themselves. 'Individual crimes were also committed by prisoners among themselves, for instance in revenge,' he testified. 'There also were many cases in which inmates thought a fellow prisoner to be a spy and killed him out of self-defence. There were cases where individual prisoners, due to physical weakness, could not keep pace with the others as regards to work and who, on top of it, aroused the disgust of the other prisoners by bad behaviour, for instance, by stealing bread or similar acts. If one considers that a large part of the prisoners were professional criminals who had already been sentenced before, it seems plausible that these people killed such fellow prisoners. This was done in many ways.'

Apart from individual crimes, Morgen also distinguished 'atrocities', caused by uncontrollable circumstances. He meant the epidemics breaking out in the camps towards the end of the war, 'caused especially by the arrival of prisoners from the Eastern areas in the concentration camps'. According to Morgen, everything was being done to control these epidemics, but still the number of victims was 'extremely high'. Something else the camp management had no control over was overpopulation. 'The prisoners arrived in a weakened condition because, due to air raids, the transports were under way longer than expected,' he explained. 'Towards the end of the war, there was a general collapse of the transportation system. Supplies could not be delivered to the necessary extent; chemical and pharmaceutical factories had been systematically bombed, and all the necessary medicines were lacking. To top all, the transports from the East further burdened the camps and crowded them in an unbearable manner.'[3]

And then, Morgen testified, there were also the 'atrocities' caused by orders from higher up. By this he meant the mass extermination of Jews, the euthanasia programme and orders from the RSHA to execute individuals and groups. The fact that Jews were systematically exterminated in the gas chambers of the extermination camps was not denied by Morgen in Nuremberg. He was never a Holocaust revisionist. In his later interview with John Toland he deemed it undeniable that during the Holocaust six million Jews had been murdered.[4] In Nuremberg he could hardly have claimed otherwise because after the testimony of Rudolph Höss, systematic genocide was a proven fact. In a naïve attempt to exonerate both himself and the SS, he attempted to attribute the responsibility for the euthanizing of the disabled as well as the extermination of the Jews exclusively to Christian Wirth. Morgen claimed that Wirth, in the execution of the euthanasia programme and the extermination of the

Jews, had not operated in the service of the SS but that he had been directly subordinate to the chancellery of the *Führer*. That is not true: although the euthanasia programme was supervised by this chancellery, the SS played an important logistic and executive role.

The SS played a major role in the extermination of the Jews, as is generally known today. The so-called *Endlösung der Judenfrage*, resulting in the systematic programme of extermination, had been handed over by Hermann Göring to the SS in the person of Reinhard Heydrich as early as 24 January 1939. It was the RSHA of the SS that supervised the *Einsatzgruppen* during the war and arranged the deportations to the extermination camps. Morgen also contended that Wirth had only been *Kriminalkommissar* in Stuttgart and not a member of the SS.[5] That Wirth had been *Kriminalkommissar* is correct but the *Kriminalpolizei* was, along with the *Gestapo*, part of the *Sicherheitspolizei*, an important branch of the SS. Wirth had enrolled in the SS as early as 1939,[6] like many of his colleagues in the police. Like all staff members of *Aktion Reinhard*, he wore an SS uniform and held an SS rank. His boss and the actual leader of the action, Odilo Globocnik, was as *SS- und Polizeiführer* subordinate to Heinrich Himmler. Morgen must have known all this; after all being an SS man himself, he worked for the *Reichskriminalpolizeiamt* and it cannot have eluded him that high-ranking officers of the *Kriminalpolizei* held a police rank in addition to a rank in the SS.

Morgen also testified about Auschwitz in Nuremberg. It is remarkable he called Auschwitz-Monowitz an extermination camp while it actually was Auschwitz-Birkenau. It is hardly likely that he was mistaken as he had visited Birkenau himself and had been taken on a lengthy tour. Probably the switch of names was part of his attempt to exonerate the SS of its responsibility for the extermination programme. He contended the SS was not responsible for Monowitz. The guards, originating from the Baltic area, charged with guarding the outer perimeter of the camp, did wear SS uniforms but did not belong to the SS, he stated. The reason they wore this uniform was 'for camouflage reasons so that this extermination camp would not be distinguished outwardly from the other labour camps and the concentration camp itself. For me as a soldier it was incomprehensible that this damage to the reputation of the SS was tolerated as it had nothing to do with this extermination.' He stated the extermination process was largely carried out by the prisoners themselves, each time under supervision of only one NCO, who wore an SS uniform as well.[7]

In reality, Monowitz, like the *Stammlager* Auschwitz and Auschwitz-Birkenau, was supervised by the SS-WVHA, the economic office of the SS. The same applied to Majdanek concentration and extermination camp in Lublin. As was usual in most concentration camps, internal security as well as camp management mostly consisted of German SS men. The Baltic guards, charged with external security, were mostly *Hilfsfreiwillige*, voluntary helpers. They may not have been fully-fledged members of the SS, but they were subordinate to Himmler. The President of the Tribunal, Sir Geoffrey Lawrence, cross-examined Morgen and exposed Morgen's transparent lie. He questioned how he could conclude that men in SS uniforms were not SS men and how could Monowitz fall outside the responsibility of the SS while SS officer Rudolph Höss was its commander? Morgen did not have a satisfactory answer to that and probably no one in the courtroom would have believed his arguments.

Morgen's testimony at the IMT could not add anything positive to the defence of the SS. The prosecution considered his answers so unconvincing it did not even want to question him. 'We do not accept his evidence as to Buchenwald, Dachau and as to conditions in concentration camps generally,' British deputy prosecutor Sir David Maxwell-Fyffe said. 'We feel, however, the Tribunal has been shown such an overwhelming amount of evidence, including films and exhibits of the consistent pattern of cruelties in the concentration camps, of the smoking chimneys of the crematoria, and of the persons who carried out these actions … .'[8]

There was indeed no shortage of evidence for the crimes committed in the concentration camps. Morgen's assertion that the SS had nothing to do with the extermination of the Jews was an outright lie, but his description of the concentration camps did contain a nucleus of truth. The facilities which Morgen described, including a brothel and a library, did indeed exist in Buchenwald, and shows and sports contests were organized for prisoners. It was not very different from many other camps; in Westerbork transit camp in the Netherlands, for instance, Jewish inmates were kept busy with sports and amusements while waiting for their deportation. It was the intention of the Westerbork camp management to put the inmates at ease so they would have no idea what terrible fate was in store for them in the East.

Better facilities were often reserved for privileged inmates. Auschwitz for instance had a brothel and inmates could swim and dive in a water basin in the camp that was used as a swimming pool. These facilities were to be used by political prisoners mainly and those holding a position within the camp hierarchy; certainly not by Jews and other inmates considered inferior. Another fact which sheds a negative light on Morgen's words is that the women and girls in the camp brothels were inmates themselves who were forced to have sex with fellow male prisoners.[9] Hence Morgen did not lie about facilities and activities in the camps, but he did try to paint a picture that did no justice to the suffering of the majority of camp prisoners; for them there was no question of a carefree life with sports and cultural activities.

The most convincing evidence of the deplorable living conditions in the concentration camps is the high number of deaths, although the prosecutors in Nuremberg did not see these statistics in sufficient perspective. They did not distinguish between concentration camp and extermination camps and did not note that living conditions and mortality figures depended on time, location and camp commander. While prisoners in extermination camps like Birkenau and Sobibor were murdered daily in large numbers in the gas chambers, prisoners in concentration camps like Buchenwald and Dachau mostly died from hunger, exhaustion, sickness or abuse by guards. There were however concentration camps with mortality rates high enough to associate them with extermination camps. For instance, in Mauthausen, 119,000 inmates out of a total of 199,404 – including 38,120 Jews – died, equal to 59.7 per cent. In Neuengamme, 55,000 out 106,000 inmates died – 51.9 per cent – and in Stutthof 65,000 out of 115,000 – 56.5 per cent.[10] As far as is known, Morgen never visited these three camps so he couldn't have witnessed the deplorable living conditions there.

In Buchenwald, the first camp visited by Morgen, some 56,000 out of a total of 238,980 – 23.4 per cent – died.[11] Of course, the official mortality figures are not completely dependable in view of the fact that in any case under Koch much tampering had been done with death certificates, but in these figures a relative decrease is evident during the period in which Morgen conducted his investigation. In 1944 – the year after Morgen had launched his investigation in the camp – the camp housed an average of 58,334 prisoners with 8,664 registered deaths – equal to 14.8 per cent. Certainly the mortality rate is higher than can be surmised from Morgen's defensive words in Nuremberg. However, this mortality rate was relatively lower than in the four preceding years. In 1940 and 1941, when Koch was still camp commander, 1,772 and 1,522 cases of death respectively were registered out of an average population of 8,290 and 7,730 – 21.4 per cent and 19.7 per cent. In 1942, 2,898 deaths were registered out of an average population of 8,784 – 33 per cent. The relative mortality rate decreased from 1943 onwards, when 3,516 deaths were registered out of an average population of 20,414 – 17.2 per cent.[12]

There are other indications as well for the improved living conditions during the post-Koch period. Buchenwald prisoner Alfred Miller stated that the conditions in the camp gradually improved from the autumn of 1943 onwards – when Morgen started his investigation. Some prisoners would even have said that from then on 'life looked like in a sanatorium'.[13] Prisoners who had been in the camp much longer and knew how bad it had been previously might have experienced it as such. In comparison to the deplorable conditions under Koch, almost any change was an improvement. This is probably also the perspective from which Morgen looked at the camp. Buchenwald was anything but a sanatorium, but while he was there the conditions were not as bad as in previous years and not so gruesome as the prosecutors in Nuremberg had envisaged after having seen all those horrible images. Forced labour, physical punishment, bad and little food and primitive living conditions always were part of camp existence, but the fact is that from about 1943 on, living conditions of non-Jewish prisoners fit for labour had relatively improved. This however was not a direct result of Morgen's efforts prosecuting sadistic camp guards but the result of the SS leadership paying much more attention at that moment to the deployment of inmates as labourers in the war industry.

Early January 1943, Richard Glücks had ordered his camp commanders 'to make every effort to decrease the mortality rate', in order 'not to endanger the prisoners' fitness for labour'.[14] Mortality rates in the camps did decrease slightly, but from the end of 1944 on, a gigantic deterioration of living conditions set in, resulting in massive numbers of deaths. The major cause was overpopulation: prisoners being evacuated from the camps in the East were being housed in the already overcrowded camps in Germany. Epidemics broke out and prisoners died from starvation in huge numbers as there was too little food available to feed all of them. In Buchenwald, 13,056 deaths were counted in the first three months of 1945; more than the two previous years combined.[15]

When the Allies liberated the concentration camps they discovered the most gruesome scenes. Weakened prisoners were lying packed close together in bunk beds in filthy, overcrowded barracks, gazing with hollow eyes into the cameras of the onrushing army photographers. Emaciated corpses were stacked outside the crematories and in Dachau a train of open railcars was standing on a side track loaded with the bodies of 2,310 prisoners who had not survived the transport from Buchenwald.[16] General Dwight Eisenhower, the Allied Commander-in-Chief on the Western Front, paid a visit to the liberated Ohrdruf camp, a satellite camp of Buchenwald, on 12 April 1945. He was shocked by what he saw: 'I have never felt able to describe my emotional reactions when I first came face to face with indisputable evidence of Nazi brutality and ruthless disregard of every shred of decency. Up to that time I had known about it only generally or through secondary sources. I am certain, however, that I have never at any other time experienced an equal sense of shock.'[17]

Graphic images of the gruesome scenes Eisenhower was talking about were distributed around the world and triggered general horror and indignation. That living conditions had not always and everywhere been so bad as in the last months of the war was a nuance no one was ready to contemplate at the time. That even Dachau made a good impression on Morgen when he visited the camp in 1944 and that it, in his words, was considered 'a very good camp', even 'a rest camp'[18] was impossible to reconcile with the image that had emerged. Morgen's description of the camps is far from representative as well, because he suppressed for instance the roll calls which lasted hours, the exhaustive forced labour and the inhuman punishments; facets that have always been part and parcel of camp life. The abuse and the crimes, attributed to individuals by Morgen, were in reality an integral part of the camp system, which had always been characterized by a total lack of rights of prisoners and disregard of human life. Dachau was no exception and with all of today's knowledge it cannot be considered as a 'rest camp' in any way; in the period the camp existed, 41,500 inmates died out of a total of around 200,000.[19]

Morgen's own experiences in the concentration camps were no complete fabrication however, as he visited the camps at a time when living conditions had been relatively improved in general and he left the camps before the gruesome chaos set in which was encountered by the Allies. Morgen probably would not have seen stacks of emaciated corpses and filthy barracks full of severely ill and starving inmates, at least not in the camps in Germany and in Vught camp. Just because Morgen's judgment is not representative of the conditions in all camps during the war, it is justified that the prosecutors rejected his testimony. Only a limited group of inmates benefitted from the temporary efforts to improve living conditions; for many it was already too late. The camps, in particular those in the East, were also the sites where the mass extermination of Jews was carried out by gassing or 'destruction by work'. Therefore the verdict of the Tribunal could not be anything else than to name the SS a criminal organization, guilty on all counts of the indictment, e.g. crimes against peace, waging a war of aggression, war crimes and crimes against humanity. This did not mean though that anyone who had been a member of the SS was automatically branded a war criminal, this had to be established individually. This was a verdict that was favourable for Morgen, as at first sight there were, except for his membership of the SS, no grounds to suspect him of war crimes.

Chapter XXIV

A One-man Crusade Against the Endlösung?

Konrad Morgen's testimony in Nuremberg was not only meant to paint a positive picture of the SS, it was also meant to save his own skin. He claimed he personally had attempted to stop the mass murder of the Jews and with success. He stated that he would, under normal circumstances, have arrested and charged Wirth and Höss after they had told him about the extermination of the Jews, but he had to tread carefully. He realized it was Hitler who 'was the instigator of these orders', and 'no military court in the world could bring the Commander-in-Chief to court, let alone the head of state'. Nonetheless, he 'did his utmost to end this operation. Hitler had to be persuaded to revoke his orders.' He realized that Himmler was the only person in a position to do something and therefore, according to himself, he spoke to numerous people who had access to the SS chief, including the chief of the *Kriminalpolizei* Arthur Nebe, Franz Breithaupt, Heinrich Müller, Oswald Pohl and *Reichsarzt SS* Ernst Robert Grawitz. However it is highly unlikely that Morgen indeed attempted to persuade these high-ranking leaders to urge Himmler to plead with Hitler to put a stop to the *Endlösung*, the extermination of the Jews.

Morgen must have known that thwarting the orders of the *Führer* openly could land him in a concentration camp or worse. There are more improbabilities in his statement. He also claimed Nebe's hair stood upright when he spoke to him: 'He was completely stunned.' Nebe could hardly have been shocked by Morgen's report about the extermination of Jews as he had been actively involved in it between June and November 1941 as commander of *Einsatzgruppe B*. Moreover, he had been in charge of experiments on the gassing of people. It cannot be said of Müller either that he knew nothing about it. He was the direct superior of Adolf Eichmann, the instigator of the deportations and he – Müller – had been extensively briefed about the extermination programme during the Wannsee conference. And Pohl also was an insider: after all his department was responsible for the extermination camps at Auschwitz-Birkenau and Majdanek. It is hardly credible that these men should have wanted to listen to a lower-ranking officer who criticized such an important order of the *Führer*. This would surely have had consequences for Morgen as well.

Here a nucleus of truth may be hidden in Morgen's testimony. He probably did speak to these leaders, but not to persuade them to put a stop to the *Endlösung*. Actually, he probably wanted to share with them his discovery of the many 'illegal' murders in the concentration camps in an attempt to win their support to be able to prosecute the perpetrators. During the Nuremberg trial, Morgen testified about a conversation he had had with Müller in the presence of Kaltenbrunner and Nebe. He claimed they talked about his plan to stop the extermination of the Jews. During the discussion, Müller had become furious and had not given Morgen any opportunity to speak. Morgen testified: 'I looked at Müller calmly, suddenly he stood up and quickly left the room, leaving me alone while the other gentlemen turned against me. In the afternoon I had a meeting with him and again told him about my views but he was still firmly against it.'

This might have been the same discussion he talked about during the Auschwitz trial in Frankfurt. However this time it was about the 'illegal' murders committed by Grabner in Auschwitz and not about stopping the extermination of the Jews. In Nuremberg, Morgen seemed to have wanted to present himself more favourably by pretending he had done all he could to end the *Endlösung*. To emphasize this he may have twisted the facts of these conversations with the department heads of the SS. Minutes have not been taken of any of these conversations; Nebe was executed by the SS at the end of the war and Müller vanished without a trace,[1] so neither could testify on this. Kaltenbrunner claimed never to have known Morgen.

Part of Morgen's testimony in Nuremberg about his alleged plan to do something against the mass murders in the concentration camps sounds more credible. Apart from having spoken with high-ranking chiefs of the SS, he would personally have taken the opportunity to 'remove from this system of destruction the leaders and important elements through the means offered by the system itself. I could not do this with regard to the killings ordered by the head of the State, but I could do it for killings outside of this order, or against this order, or for other serious crimes.' By attempting to prosecute for instance Höss or Wirth for corruption, 'illegal murders' and other crimes, he hoped to thwart the extermination programme to such an extent that it would lead to the 'final collapse of the system'. It has been firmly established that Morgen did set himself to prosecuting individual participants in the extermination programme, not letting himself be deterred by intimidation and counteracts from higher up. Neither were there any indications he supported the anti-Semitism of the party, nor was he an advocate of the extermination of the Jews. However, he must have realized that the arrest of a few individuals was only a drop in the ocean: the extermination programme was unstoppable. After all, within the system of extermination everybody except Hitler was expendable. Had he had Höss arrested, a large amount of expertise would have been lost, but a successor would have been appointed. Moreover, Morgen knew from experience that whenever he wanted to prosecute an influential person, the chances were more than even that Himmler would put his foot down. Morgen's authority was limited by the principle within the SS that not the law but the will of Himmler and Hitler was the decisive factor.

In Nuremberg, Morgen claimed nonetheless that his efforts to stop the mass murders were partially successful. 'The killing system was severely shaken,' he stated proudly. He referred to the alleged fact that Wirth 'suddenly received orders to completely destroy all his extermination camps'.[2] The closure of Belzec, Sobibor and Treblinka had nothing to do however with Morgen's investigation: the reality is that the camps were closed for the simple but gruesome reason that almost all Jews in the General Government had been exterminated, effectively ending *Aktion Reinhard*. As the capacity of the gas chambers in Auschwitz was sufficient for killing the remaining European Jews, Belzec, Sobibor and Treblinka had become redundant. Morgen also claimed: 'The immediate effects of the judicial investigation were that in all concentration camps the killing of prisoners by so-called "euthanasia" stopped immediately, because no doctor could feel sure that he would not be arrested from one moment to the next. I am convinced that through this intervention and action the lives of thousands of prisoners were saved.'[3]

The euthanasia of prisoners was carried out under the code 14f13 and was largely done in the institutions previously used for euthanizing the disabled in connection with *Aktion T4*. A total of 10,000 to 20,000 prisoners would fall victim to 14f13. The operation was indeed officially suspended in 1943, but Morgen was not responsible for that either. Himmler stopped the operation because he felt it was no longer expedient to kill prisoners who were fit for labour. From then on, only the mentally disabled were to be selected for euthanasia. All these centres were closed down except Hartheim in Austria where some 3,000 inmates from Mauthausen and Gusen concentration camps were murdered in 1944.[4] Although Morgen claimed otherwise, never at any moment did his investigation have any influence on the execution of the euthanasia and extermination programmes.

In his later interview for *The World at War*, Morgen was a lot more realistic about his role during the war. He said that Auschwitz was 'a horrible experience' for him, so he 'made plans to sneak across the border into Switzerland'. He decided not to do so as he feared nobody would believe him when he talked about the gas chambers. 'I could hardly believe my own eyes and ears when I saw it for the first time.' Moreover, he was afraid he would be mistaken for an 'agent-provocateur, a spy or a lunatic. It would only lead to great suffering for myself or my parents. And that was senseless because I could not change anything.' Subsequently he thought up the following plan: 'Although I cannot catch those responsible for the extermination of millions of people, the least I can do is to bring to court those among the executors who have strayed from the so-called path of legality for having acted of their own accord in order to enrich themselves, having attempted to cover up their crimes or acted out of greed for power or out of any other motive they might have had to apply violence to prisoners. I can indict them for these sorts of things, to get those monsters behind bars and put an end to their misdeeds.' He understood very well that he could not change an entire system, 'especially when there is a war on'.[5] This statement is much more credible than what he stated in Nuremberg. It may very well be this explanation was the truth.

The story Morgen told in Nuremberg was believed by some. One of them was American historian and Pulitzer prize winner John Toland. In his biography of Adolf Hitler, published in 1976, he wrote about Morgen's 'lonely efforts to put an end to the *Endlösung*' and concluded that Morgen's 'one-man crusade had a destructive effect on the extermination facility in

Lublin. *Kriminalkommissar* Wirth was ordered to destroy, without leaving a trace, three of the four camps he had established: Treblinka, Sobibor and Belzec.[6] Toland also wrote that on 24 November 1944 Himmler ordered the extermination centres to be closed 'incited by the speedy advance of the Red Army and the continuing investigations by the tenacious Konrad Morgen'.[7] Toland based his assertions largely on the interview he had had with Morgen of which a sound recording has been preserved. Toland's fascination for Morgen's judicial investigation in the concentration camps is evident in this interview. He voiced his puzzlement that there was 'any justice' in the Third Reich. 'Many people in the West would not believe this,' he told Morgen.

Toland appeared amazed that Morgen had never received recognition after the war for the work he had done in the camps, risking his life in the process.[8] But the American hardly asked critical questions and perhaps let himself be impressed too much by Morgen's story.

A one-man crusade was entirely out of the question as Morgen worked with a team of investigators and sentencing lay in the hands of the SS and police courts supervised by *Gerichtsherren* with Himmler and Hitler as supreme judges. Toland made a connection between the abolition of the extermination programme and Morgen's investigation, but did not substantiate this with evidence. Just as the camps of *Aktion Reinhard* were not closed because of Morgen, neither had the closure of Auschwitz actually anything to do with Morgen. The murder factory in Auschwitz was closed as late as November 1944. The only reason for Himmler to order the destruction of the crematories in Birkenau was that he wanted to hide all traces of the mass extermination from the relentlessly advancing Red Army. Shortly before the liberation of the camp on 27 January, a few hundred prisoners were executed by the SS, but there had not been time enough to kill all remaining inmates.[9] The survivors of Auschwitz owed their lives to the fast-approaching Red Army, not to an SS judge.

Chapter XXV

I Was Just an Administrator

On the heels of the International Military Tribunal, twelve trials were also held in Nuremberg between 9 December 1946 and 13 April 1949 before an American military tribunal. There were cases against, for instance, staff members of the chemical plant IG Farben, commanders of the *Einsatzgruppen*, and high-ranking officers of the *Oberkommando der Wehrmacht*. From 8 April to 3 November 1947 the case against Oswald Pohl and seventeen staff members of his *SS-Wirtschafts und Verwaltungshauptamt* (SS-WVHA) was down for hearing. Born on 30 June 1892, the former paymaster in the German *Kriegsmarine* was recruited by Himmler in 1934 to 'reorganize the administration and financial management of the SS'. He 'managed to rebuild the SS, rejuvenating its administration with efficient bookkeeping and financial departments'. Eventually he rose to the rank of *SS-Obergruppenführer* and, as the head of the SS-WVHA, established in 1942, he was one of the most powerful men in the SS. His bureau was much more than a managerial office and also handled the organization of building projects, provisioning of the *Waffen-SS*, and the management of factories, agricultural enterprises and mining.

Amt D of the SS-WVHA, headed by the Inspector of the concentration camps Richard Glücks, was responsible for the management of the concentration camps, including the allocation of inmates as forced labourers to the German war industry. The bureau was also tasked with the logistic coordination of the confiscated properties of the victims in the extermination camps, including the gold teeth. It entailed 'mainly valuables of the Jews' that were collected by the SS-WVHA, Pohl told prison psychiatrist Leon Goldensohn after the war. He knew the former owners had been killed and he assumed 'some of the gold bars I had received consisted of the melted gold teeth'. He evaded all responsibility though: 'I never ordered to take away these things … they just happened to be there and I had to take them to the *Reichsbank* and that is what I did. I never inspected the gold teeth and bridges myself as I was too busy with other matters.'[1]

Pohl never told Goldensohn that he had issued an order on 16 August 1942, reading: 'In all concentration and extermination camps, the hair cut off from women is to be collected. After it has been combed and cut, the women's hair can be made into slippers for U-boat crews and felt socks for *Reichsbahn* personnel.'[2] He must have known that most of the hair originated from Jewish women who had been killed in the gas chambers when he issued this order, but he played dumb towards Goldensohn and evaded all responsibility. He did admit however to have known about the extermination of the Jews and acknowledged that the concentration camps – hence also Auschwitz-Birkenau and Majdanek – formally fell within his authority, but he denied having taken part in the murder of the Jews: 'I had nothing to do with the *Endlösung* of the Jews. That was carried out by the personnel of the camps such as the commanders. Of course, Gestapo-Müller was the central figure of all those orders to exterminate the Jews. He got his orders from Kaltenbrunner who carried out Himmler's plans.'

Pohl shifted the blame to Richard Glücks, who had been his subordinate, but he 'did not receive the orders, pertaining to the extermination programme, from me but straight from Müller'. Pohl did not feel 'responsible in any way for or guilty of the murder of five million Jews or the death of others in the concentration camps. … I was just an administrator.'[3] He maintained this defence during his trial in Nuremberg where he and his colleagues were indicted for having participated in a conspiracy to commit war crimes, for having committed war crimes and crimes against humanity, and membership of a criminal organization. The indictment of the American tribunal read: 'These crimes included murders, brutalities, cruelties, tortures, atrocities, deportations, enslavement, forced labour, plunder of property, and other inhuman and unlawful acts.'[4]

On 21 and 22 August 1947, Konrad Morgen was subpoenaed to testify as witness for the defence during the trial against Pohl and his subordinates. It is remarkable he testified in favour of the man he later described as corrupt and whom he blamed for having obstructed his investigation. Morgen's previous testimony before the IMT matched well with the speech of Pohl's counsel, Dr Alfred Seidel. In his opening speech

Seidel indicated that Pohl had also been indicted for 'responsibility for and participation in the so-called final solution of the Jewish question'. Seidel argued however that the SS-WVHA had had nothing to do with the extermination of the Jews and referred to Morgen's testimony of a year earlier in which he claimed that the mass murder of the Jews had been carried out by Wirth and a small group of associates and not by the SS as a whole. In his turn, Seidel shifted the blame to Adolf Eichmann and Odilo Globocnik and stated that 'the extermination camps at Treblinka, Belzec, Majdanek and others did not belong to the domain of the inspector of the concentration camps'. In his words, the SS-WVHA was just a management office without executive branches, so because of that alone, Pohl could not be guilty of any count of the indictment.[5] In his closing speech, Pohl's counsel again referred to Morgen's testimony and repeated once more that the extermination camp fell outside the responsibility of Pohl's offices. Seidel declared: 'The circle of persons charged with the so-called final solution of the Jewish problem was strictly limited and very small,' and that the SS-WVHA 'had nothing to do with the actual execution of these tasks at any time'.[6]

In his defence, Oswald Pohl also referred to Morgen. In his final statement on 22 September 1947 he claimed he had attempted to keep the conditions in the concentration camps bearable out of humane considerations. He was 'genuinely sorry his efforts have been denied an appropriate success'. He claimed he could do nothing about it; after all it was impossible for him to 'to supervise personally this entire organization from a ministerial level in Berlin'. He also put the blame on 'the mess in the traffic and supply situation which was caused by the destructive air attacks of the Allies'. He testified: 'Wherever I met deficiencies I fought them energetically.' One of these deficiencies was, in his words, Morgen's activities. Pohl claimed he had initially approved of Morgen's investigation in the camps, but eventually he had to reject them 'when I realized that, in spite of the highest authority and the greatest support from highest sources, he did not succeed in introducing rapid and exemplary justice in the extermination of the pest of atrocities in the concentration camps. In his place, the institution of a special court was welcomed by me and thoroughly supported.'[7] Morgen being hardly successful though was largely Pohl's fault. He had always hindered the investigation by Morgen and his colleagues. Later on Morgen would testify about it and so did

Dr Grünther Reinecke during the Nuremberg trial. Reinecke declared: 'Outwardly he pretended to welcome and support with all means the investigating work of the head office "SS Courts". ... In reality, Pohl sabotaged the investigations we were making and with all the means of his tremendously powerful position worked hand in glove with the detainees and the criminal commanders, as we proved on the basis of evidence.'[8]

During the trial Morgen's testimony met distrust again. He denied for instance the existence of a gas chamber in Dachau, to which one of the judges reacted: 'We know about the false shower bath, and we know about the crematoria, so don't try to tell us there were no exterminations at Dachau. ... There is not any question about it.' Morgen replied: 'The presence of a crematory does not necessarily prove that people were being gassed before being taken to the crematory.'[9] Morgen was right, there was no systematic mass extermination in Dachau; the crematory was mainly used to cremate the corpses of prisoners who had not died from gassing but for instance from disease or starvation. Contrary to what he claimed, Dachau did possess a gas chamber suitable for killing people, although it was probably used on an experimental scale only.[10]

The tribunal also took a critical view of Morgen's criminal investigation in the concentration camps. Judge Michael A. Musmanno proclaimed that the German population should be informed of 'all arrogance, conceit, pusillanimity, and brutality' the SS uniform stood for. 'The tinsel trappings must be torn away and the SS revealed in all its shamelessness and greed. The German people must know the SS scale of values.' He pointed out that Morgen in the case against Koch drafted his indictments in this sequence: 'first, embezzlement and disloyalty; and second, murder. To the SS hierarchy human life was not as important as money and what it stands for.'[11]

The facts were to Pohl's disadvantage. The court ruled: 'Pohl at all times had an intimate and detailed knowledge of happenings in any way connected with the concentration camps. He knew how many prisoners died; he knew how many were unfit for work ... . There was doubtless no other one person in Germany who knew as much about all the details of the concentration camps as Pohl.' His assertion that not he but Richard Glücks was responsible for the concentration camps and the crimes committed there was rejected by the judges. 'Pohl cannot escape the fact that he was the administrative head of the agency which brought about these tragedies. His was more than a mere consenting part. It was active participation. Leaving all other considerations aside, Pohl stands before this Tribunal as an admitted slave driver on a scale never before known.'

The SS-WVHA may not have been responsible for the management and personnel of the extermination camps at Belzec, Chełmno, Sobibor and Treblinka, but for Auschwitz-Birkenau and Majdanek it was. Moreover, the SS-WVHA had played an important role in the confiscation of the possessions of the victims of the extermination camps. 'The fact that Pohl himself did not actually transport the stolen goods to the Reich or did not himself remove the gold from the teeth of dead inmates, does not exonerate him. This was a broad criminal programme, requiring the cooperation of many persons, and Pohl's part was to conserve and account for the loot. Having knowledge of the illegal purposes of the action and of the crimes which accompanied it, his active participation even in the after phases of the action make him *particeps criminis* in the whole affair.'[12] Pohl was found guilty of war crimes, crimes against humanity and membership of a criminal organization. On 3 November 1947 he was sentenced to death by hanging.[13] The execution was postponed pending new evidence that might shed new light on the Pohl case, but it didn't. The death sentence was not revised and was carried out on 7 June 1951. Initially three other defendants in the same case were sentenced to death, but in 1948 and 1951 their sentence was reduced to imprisonment. Three defendants were acquitted as early as 1947, seven were granted amnesty in 1951, and eventually seven convicts served sentences from eight to twenty years.[14]

Chapter XXVI

From Prime Suspect to Fellow-traveller

On 28 January 1946, Konrad Morgen was taken into political custody in the *Internierungslager* Ludwigsburg in Baden-Württemberg. Because he had been a member of the NSDAP and had held a high rank in the SS, he was subjected to a denazification trial. This was part of a programme of denazification – *Entnazifizierung* – set up by the Allies. The goal was a political cleansing of post-war Germany to prevent the National Socialists from ever seizing power again. Special courts, so-called *Spruchkammer*, manned by German judges, were established to determine how big someone's role in the Nazi regime had been. There were five categories, each with appropriate penalties: the first and most severe category was that of the *Hauptschuldige* or the prime suspects. Defendants in this category could be sentenced to death or life imprisonment. Party activists, militarists and profiteers were grouped in the second category, the *Belastete* – suspects – and faced sentences up to a maximum of ten years. The third category was that of the *Minderschuldige*, or lesser suspects, consisting of, for instance, young male party members who had been in military service. Defendants in this category could count on a suspended sentence of two to three years. Then there was category four, the *Mitläufer* or fellow-travellers, entailing low-ranking party members who had neither taken an active part in party activities nor in the war. They were placed under surveillance by the police and obliged to pay a fine. Acquittal was reserved for those grouped in the fifth category, the *Nichtbelastete* or *Entlastete*, the innocent. They were former members of the NSDAP who had actively or passively resisted National Socialism or had suffered from it.

On 9 June 1948, the public prosecutor of the *Spruchkammer* in Ludwigsburg put in a claim for Konrad Morgen to be sentenced to *Hauptschuldige*. He was not accused of individual crimes, but because of his role within the DAF and in particular his work as SS judge, it was, according to the prosecutor, 'a case of extraordinary support of the

National Socialist dictatorship'. The case was opened on 24 June 1948 and chaired by the president of the court, *Justizoberinspektor* Meyer. Morgen conducted a fiery defence: he said he had become a lawyer to 'serve justice' and pressed upon the court that he had fought against 'crimes against humanity'. He claimed to have entered service in the SS involuntarily and that he had only been a candidate member of the *Allgemeine-SS*. He described Himmler, whom he had called 'a great man with a sensitive heart' before the war, as a 'man of violence' who knew no justice. The higher SS leadership had, in his opinion, 'a double morality'. His work had entailed great risk, but he claimed that it was he who had provoked Himmler to issue the order that inmates were not to be tortured anymore and political prisoners not be used for experiments. He ended with: 'I have stood up for those who suffered or were in pain. With this, I swallowed a damned hot potato; I did more than my duty. I have acted against the violence, against the injustice and high-handedness and prosecuted the guilty. I am not a fellow-traveller, but from the beginning of my public career, I have rowed against the current.'

He received support from Alfred Miller, the prisoner who had testified for him in the Koch case during the war. Miller stated he owed his release from Buchenwald to Morgen. He also argued Morgen had taken a huge risk by launching an investigation into the SS men in Buchenwald. Morgen could have suffered the same fate as camp guard Köhler who had been poisoned. Miller stated further that living conditions in Buchenwald had improved as a result of Morgen's actions.

The denazification court, consisting of a professional presiding judge and four lay judges, held that the charge of 'extraordinary support of National Socialism as well as having held an executive position' was unproved. Nonetheless, it indicated that Morgen, like all the other SS judges, had to be sentenced as *Hauptschuldige*, as demanded by the public prosecutor. However, it waived this for various reasons. According to the court, the defendant had not occupied himself with political issues but with crimes against property 'like those that would be prosecuted in any democratic state'. Thereby he had strictly adhered to the law. 'He has thereby followed the ethics of a truth-finding judge to the utmost and fulfilled the duty of a meticulous representative of justice.' The court established that Morgen had not only 'displayed the courage to engage the highest SS officers', but that he also 'had put up active resistance'. He had fought against the violence in the concentration camps 'with all his energy'. In doing so, the living conditions in the camp had been improved. Thus the court accepted the testimony of witness Miller.

Miller's argument that Morgen risked being killed by SS colleagues, as guard Köhler had been, was also accepted. Reference was made not only to the risk he took of being murdered, but also to that of being discharged, as had actually occurred in 1942 as a result of his refusal to obey an order of Himmler in the case against the policeman who had been charged with sexual intercourse with a Polish woman. 'He has put his life on the line and followed the road of a judge undeterred,' the court ruled. The prosecutor waived his previous charge and now proposed that Morgen be designated a *Mitläufer*. However, due to his alleged resistance against the crimes in the concentration camps and the risks he took in the process, the court finally decided to classify him as *Entlastete*. After three years Morgen was a free man again and the state was ordered to pay the fees.[1]

In 1950 Morgen was to account for himself again before a *Spruchkammer*, this time in Nord-Württemberg. The case was held in connection with the *Gesetz zum Abschluss der politischen Befreiung* – law to end political liberation – of 3 April 1950. This law was meant to end the programme of denazification in order to prevent culprits slipping through holes in the net or being sentenced unlawfully. In Morgen's case the Ministry had called for a revision, as judicial complaints had been lodged against his acquittal. 'The *Spruchkammer* had omitted the fact that in the actions of defendant, there is no question of active resistance against the National Socialist dictatorship.' His great efforts in fighting corruption and crimes within the SS had been 'made in his capacity as SS judge and it has not been proven his actions had possibly been directed against the National Socialist regime.' In the opinion of the Ministry, it looked more like he had only occupied himself 'with cleansing measures within the ranks of the SS'. Therefore Morgen's political responsibility had to be reassessed in light of the fact that he had been promoted to *SS-Sturmbannführer* in the *Waffen-SS* as late as November 1944. In other words: someone with such a high rank should, according to the Ministry, not have been acquitted on grounds of alleged resistance activities.

The indictment against Morgen was milder than the point of view of the Ministry. As in 1946, it was established during the trial that he wasn't guilty of individual incriminating facts. Although Morgen had, according to the indictment, enrolled voluntarily in the *Allgemeine-SS* he had never occupied a position within the party and had kept the relatively low rank of *SS-Rottenführer* until the outbreak of the war; all subsequent promotions had taken place in connection with his function as SS judge, not as executive in the SS. In his case there was, again according to the indictment, no question of special or substantial support of the party, nor was he considered a dedicated follower of the National Socialist dictatorship. In contrast, it was considered proven that he had taken a stand against the crimes of the SS and suffered personal damage because of his attitude. It was also indicated that he had voluntarily reported as a witness in Nuremberg and consequently had contributed to the sentencing of the defendants. This assertion is questionable though, as in Nuremberg he was a witness for the defence, not for the prosecution. Whatever it was, it was demanded that no change be made to Morgen's previous acquittal. If the court could not agree however, the prosecution stated that Morgen could be designated a *Mitläufer* at most.

In its verdict of 27 November 1950, the court adopted most of the points in the indictment. 'Defendant has not played a leading role within the *Allgemeine-SS* and the *Waffen-SS*,' the court concluded. His work as SS judge was not deemed incriminating either, as SS courts could not be compared to party courts but to military courts of the *Wehrmacht* that applied the general law of war. A dubious conclusion, in view of the subjection of the courts to Himmler and the National Socialist ideology. As to Morgen himself, he did not let himself be led by Himmler but by the military penal code. The case against the policeman in Poland in 1942 is a clear example. The court considered Morgen's actions against the crimes of the SS a mitigating factor. Neither was his work for the DAF considered incriminating. He was considered 'just a nominal party member who supported the NSDAP on and off'. This time he was not placed in the *Entlastete* category but was considered a *Mitläufer*. Morgen pleaded to be categorized as *Entlastete* again however, because of his actions against the crimes of the SS and his active resistance against the National Socialist dictatorship. But his plea was rejected. In practice it did not matter though, because pursuant to the new legislation, judicial distinction between categories three to five no longer existed.[2] Hence the revised verdict of the *Spruchkammer* had no influence on Morgen's life.

Chapter XXVII

A Paradoxical Result in Frankfurt

After his denazification trials were over, Morgen resumed his pre-war career. He became a counsel in Frankfurt am Main. From 16 May 1951 until 19 January 1979 he was a member of the local *Rechtsanwaltkammer* – bar association.[1] In this period he acted again as a witness during a trial against war criminals, namely the first Auschwitz trial that took place in Frankfurt from 10 December 1963 to 10 August 1965.[2] The trial was not held by an international or American military tribunal but by the West German judicature itself. Indicted were twenty-one SS men and a Kapo who had worked in Auschwitz. It was not the first trial dedicated entirely to crimes in Auschwitz as forty-one staff members of the camp had been tried by a Polish tribunal in Krakow between 24 November 1943 and 22 December 1947. One of the defendants there was Arthur Liebehenschel, who had been camp commander of the *Stammlager* in Auschwitz from November 1943 until May 1944. He was sentenced to death and executed, along with twenty others. Nineteen defendants were sentenced to prison terms varying from three years to life. One person was acquitted.[3] The sentences in Frankfurt were much lighter, but that was not caused by a shortage of witnesses. Over a period of 22 months and 183 sessions, over 350 witnesses were heard including 211 survivors of Auschwitz.[4] Among the witnesses there were only a few SS men. They had refused to cooperate in fear of being prosecuted themselves, and anyway their testimonies were considered unreliable. Apart from Morgen, his former colleagues Gerhard Wiebeck and Wilhelm Reimers testified as well, albeit the latter during the preliminary hearings only and not during the trial itself.

The trial in Frankfurt was massively attended by the international press and grew into a media show. The trial was important for the awareness of young Germans of the crimes committed by the generation of their parents or grandparents. Initially it took place in the large auditorium in the town hall, but in April 1964 the sessions were moved to the newly constructed

Gallus community centre which had enough room to accommodate 87 participants in the trial, an audience of 143, and 124 representatives of the press. Among the defendants were those who had played an active role in the extermination camps, such as Joseph Klehr who had been responsible for gassing with *Zyklon-B* and had killed prisoners by phenol injections in the heart. A news bulletin by German television of the first session in Haus Gallus showed the defendants arriving in police vans with emergency lights flashing. When the men got out of the vans, they used their briefcases to hide their faces from the cameras. An irascible defendant used his bag to strike at the intrusive journalists who had assembled in front of the building. As if the men were liable to flee, a massive police force was assembled in the courtroom.[5] The defendants did not pose a real threat anymore, but during the war things had been very different. One of the defendants for instance was Wilhelm Boger, inventor of the 'Boger swing'. Morgen had tried to get him convicted during the war but had failed. Morgen might have been expected to welcome this new opportunity to convict this 'beast', but his demeanour did not match that of a witness who was out for justice.

Canadian historian Rebecca Wittmann wrote a book about the Auschwitz trial in Frankfurt and dealt with Morgen's role as a witness. During both the preliminary and the official hearings he said remarkably little about the defendants. When he was first examined on 8 March 1962 by investigative judge Dr Heinz Düx, he could not recall anything about defendant Franz Johann Hofmann who had guided him through the camp. He was not sure at all whether he had launched an investigation into defendant Boger on suspicion of corruption and murder, nor could he remember anything about the trial against Maximilian Grabner in Weimar during the war.[6] In court he knew little about the 'Boger swing', seeming to be unaware that it was an illegal torture tool. Only after it was pointed out to him did he recall that defendant Joseph Klehr had been involved in 'something illegal', namely killing prisoners by injecting phenol into their hearts. When Judge Hofmeyer asked about the legality of these injections, he declared that these injections were legal only when the victims were incurably ill. He also said that Klehr had drafted falsified death certificates but he, Morgen, did not know more.

Judge Hofmeyer was irritated by Morgen during the sessions as he seemed able to recall so little. Morgen then addressed him and the other judges as colleagues and argued it was difficult to remember something that happened twenty years ago. 'You as fellow judges should understand this.'[7] There was some truth in that, as during the war Morgen had visited numerous concentration camps, had handled many different cases and spoken to many suspects. It is conspicuous though that at the same time he was perfectly able to give a detailed description of the crematory annex gas chamber he had visited. He remembered exactly what the terrain outside the building was covered with, what was on the notice boards in the dressing rooms and how the building was subdivided. It cannot be assumed he wanted to protect the defendants in Frankfurt in view of the fact that during the war he had prosecuted SS men for similar crimes himself. Probably he only wanted to avoid becoming known as a traitor, or was afraid of damaging his reputation as a lawyer by mentioning too many incriminating facts about the defendants. After all, it was his job to defend suspects, not prosecute them.

While Morgen's testimony was rejected in Nuremberg, it did play a significant role in Frankfurt. He managed to explain to the court what, pursuant to Nazi legislation, was a crime and what not in the concentration camps. He stressed that the gassing of Jews was 'simply the carrying out of orders', but that he had also discovered that many executions took place in the camps that were not carried out on orders from above but out of personal motives. When the judge asked him what was accepted in the field of torture, he quoted the camp rules, causing visible irritation among the audience in the courtroom who rejected these rules. Judge Hofmeyer also asked if the military penal code was applied in the Third Reich, in particular paragraph 47 which laid down that an order to commit a crime should not be obeyed. Morgen confirmed that this rule was formally valid, but that it was difficult to determine, under the prevailing circumstances of the time, what exactly was a crime. According to him, a political decision was not to be criticized by a soldier. Hofmeyer acknowledged this but stated: 'There can be no discussion about whether or not a soldier should follow an order to throw innocent little children into burning fires. It must be clear to a soldier that this is a crime.' Morgen agreed with him but said he could not imagine 'that kind of thing happened, because it contradicts the entire direction [of the Nazi regime]'. In his opinion, individual murder and sadism did not match the nature of a 'true German'. He declared: 'Despite everything that everyone says about them, despite everything that happened, the SS never ordered or demanded such cruelties.'[8]

The testimonies of Morgen's former colleagues Gerhard Wiebeck and Wilhelm Reimers were very similar to his own. During the preliminary hearing, Reimers declared that he had conducted investigations into 'illegal murdering of prisoners' committed in the political branch of Auschwitz during the war, but he pointed out to his interrogator that '*Judenaktionen*' were not included. He was only ordered to investigate 'illegal theft' of Jewish possessions. He admitted having witnessed executions but had not been able to prevent them 'because my power of authority did not reach that far. It was my duty to establish what was going on in Auschwitz and report about it.' Reimers also said he had witnessed the arrival of transports and the subsequent gassings. He gave a factual description, seemingly without remorse or abhorrence. The prisoners who had been gassed looked peaceful to him 'as if they had died a natural death'. Wiebeck testified in court that 'investigation into general murders was not permitted. I learned that the order to exterminate the Jews had been given verbally by Hitler.' The gassings were not investigated by him or his colleagues. 'That didn't interest us at that time. Those were "supreme acts beyond justice" [*justizfreie Hoheitsakte*].'[9]

As he had done in Nuremberg, during this Auschwitz trial Morgen painted an image of the SS based only on the theory of the law. He again presented himself as a determined and courageous defender of justice while in Nazi ideology real justice was lacking. Although it was not policy imposed from above to throw children into the fire, or to kill healthy prisoners by injections in the heart, or to torture Jews before they were murdered in the gas chambers, it did happen nonetheless. Those crimes were the inevitable consequence of the orders with which the SS burdened its staff members. The extermination of Jews and supervising prisoners who were considered inferior brought out the worst in them. It shows Morgen's hypocrisy that he considered that throwing children into the fire did not match the norms and values of 'real' Germans and of the SS, as he knew full well that Germans and members of the SS were responsible for the systematic extermination of millions of innocent people. The fact that these crimes were ordered by the state, in the person of Hitler, does in no way mitigate the personal guilt of everyone involved in this genocide, although the court in Frankfurt would eventually rule otherwise.

In contrast to Allied military tribunals trying Nazi criminals for war crimes and crimes against humanity the defendants in Frankfurt were tried in accordance with the regular West German penal code.[10] During the trial the principle of legality was applied, meaning that defendants could only be pronounced guilty of violating laws which had been effective in the period in which they committed their crimes: hence in this case in accordance with the laws of Nazi Germany. This meant none of the defendants could be indicted for genocide or crimes against humanity because in the pre-1945 penal code these crimes did not exist. Instead they were indicted for murder or complicity to murder. Others, of whom it could only be established that they had cooperated in the extermination programme, were pronounced guilty of 'mutual cooperation with collective murder' and received relatively much lighter sentences than those of whom it could be established they had murdered prisoners on their own initiative. Those men had also violated the law that was valid at the time, while the men who had participated in the extermination programme had 'simply' carried out orders.

Thanks, however, to the information of Morgen and his colleagues, it could be proved that Boger and Klehr were individually guilty of multiple murder and they were sentenced to life. This was the most severe penalty possible as capital punishment had been abolished in the German Federal Republic as early as 1949. Four other defendants received a life sentence as well, and eleven were given sentences varying from three years and three months to fourteen years. Two defendants were released during the trial and three were acquitted for reasons of health although it had been proved they had worked in Auschwitz and hence were part of the systematic mass murder. After a revision one of those sentenced to imprisonment was acquitted as late as 1970.[11]

The decision of the court to penalize individual murder more severely than cooperation with the extermination programme was an echo of the principle Morgen had had to adhere to in Nazi Germany. Critics claimed the court had lent a certain legitimacy to the laws of the Nazi era and simultaneously to the extermination programme. Rebecca Wittmann concluded in her book that the Auschwitz trial in Frankfurt resulted in a paradox. She writes:

'On the one hand, it illuminated the crimes of Auschwitz for a public that was almost completely – and often deliberately – ignorant of them. ... On the other hand, the public also gained a skewed understanding of Auschwitz. The sentences meted out to the defendants distorted the realities of the programme of extermination at Auschwitz. ... The statements of the judges about the brutality of such defendants as Wilhelm Boger, the 'Devil of Birkenau', shifted the focus in the courtroom away from Nazi genocide towards individual acts of cruelty, suggesting that, in formal legal terms at least, the Nazi orders had been acceptable: those who had herded thousands into the gas chambers were not as guilty as those who had shot prisoners without having had a legal death sentence handed down by Nazi officials in Berlin. Defendants who had selected prisoners for death on the platform benefited from such a distortion of justice: they were convicted only of aiding and abetting murder.'[12]

When John Iwan Demjanjuk, a war criminal born in the Ukraine, was convicted by the court in Munich in 2011, the simple fact that someone had been employed as a guard in an extermination camp led to a conviction in Germany for the first time. It was no longer required to prove the defendant had been guilty of individual crimes. The fact that Demjanjuk was employed in the Sobibor extermination camp at the time genocide took place there was sufficient reason to sentence the 91-year-old to five years in prison for the murder of 27,900 Jews.[13]

Chapter XXVIII

From Lawyer and Witness to Defendant

After the war Konrad Morgen was involved with the court system not only as a witness and a lawyer but also as defendant. Three times the *Landesgericht* in Frankfurt launched a preliminary investigation into a case against him. These investigations were started by the public prosecutor, although the *Spruchkammer* had already acquitted him of individual crimes. The charges related to two crimes Morgen allegedly committed during the war. The preliminary investigation was launched in 1955. Morgen was suspected of having drafted an appeal to the Hungarian Jews who were to be deported to Auschwitz in 1944, which read something like:

'Jewish men and women!

Do not be afraid, nothing will happen to you in Germany. You will be deployed to work there as Germany needs the labour of every man and every woman. Do not throw away your valuables, do not hand them over to the Hungarian police but take them with you to Germany instead. You will perhaps need them there.'

Most of the Hungarian Jews were not deployed for work but gassed in Auschwitz. The text in this pamphlet was comparable to what was used to put Jews all over Europe at ease prior to their deportation, in order that the transports proceeded without problems. Consequently Morgen was suspected of having 'supported the deportation and murder of the Hungarian Jews'. Morgen acknowledged he had been in Budapest for two days at the time to interrogate Adolf Eichmann, the organizer of the deportations. He did deny however that he had drafted a pamphlet with such a message. He admitted though that he had become aware of 'guards and accompanying men of the transports using their authority to take money and valuables away from the victims'. Hence he deemed it possible that 'he had urged – possibly in the form of a memorandum – to point out to the deportees that guards are not authorized to confiscate money and valuables'. He would not have done so to contribute to the smooth progress of the deportations but to lend a little support to the deportees. The court doubted his explanation. 'The request to the Hungarian Jews to embark without fear for their trip to Germany does indicate that the resistance of the victims against their deportation would be weakened. Therefore, it looks like defendant has supported the deportation and with it the murder of the Jews.'

Nevertheless, Morgen was acquitted by the court as 'it was impossible to prove whether the appeal had actually been issued and that defendant had supported the deportation and the subsequent murder of the Jews'. No indications were found either as to why Morgen would have supported the murder of the Jews. An 'interrogation of the former Zionist leader in Hungary, Dr Rudolf Kastner, could not produce any clarification of the facts'. It was not expected either that Dr Kastner would confirm there had been Jews who had given up their initial refusal to be deported because of this appeal.[1]

In 1972 Morgen was indicted for the same reason but again to no avail. He declared he 'had never at any moment given support to the Hungarian Jews and in particular had nothing to do whatsoever with drafting and issuing said pamphlet'. In the archives, no evidence has been found and declarations by witnesses did not contain any incriminating information. Moreover, former *SS-Obersturmbannführer* and SS judge Kurt Mittelstädt, the witness who had connected Morgen to the pamphlet, had passed away. 'Therefore, the responsibility of defendant Dr Morgen cannot be proven.'[2]

Whether or not Morgen was responsible or co-responsible for the draft of the pamphlet remains vague, but it is certain he stayed in Hungary for a short while in 1944, as he admitted himself. He would have been there to hear Adolf Eichmann, who was suspected of the theft of 'a few valuable watches, other valuables and stock from a safe in Berlin'.[3] During the Nuremberg trial, Morgen confirmed he had been in Hungary at the time. He claimed he had travelled there to arrest Eichmann. This had, so he testified, been thwarted by Ernst Kaltenbrunner, chief of the RSHA and Eichmann's *Gerichtsherr*. When Morgen asked Kaltenbrunner for an arrest warrant for Eichmann, he called in Heinrich Müller immediately. Subsequently Morgen was told an arrest was not contemplated as 'Eichmann carried out a special, secret task of the greatest importance, entrusted to him by the *Führer*'.[4]

It cannot be excluded that Morgen urged the organizers of the deportations from Hungary to inform the Jews they should not hand their valuables over to the corrupt guards on the trains and Hungarian police officers. He certainly did not do so to lend a little support to the Jews, knowing their final destination and that their possessions would be taken from them in Auschwitz anyway to be transferred to the *Reichsbank*. Nor did he do this to have the deportations proceed quietly, as it was not in his interest to do so. The only plausible reason he could have done so was to prevent corruption, which had been his mission all along.

The other preliminary investigation against Morgen was conducted in 1961. At the time, he was charged with involvement in the death of four Soviet prisoners-of-war in camp Buchenwald in 1943. The indictment was based on a text in the book *Der SS Staat* by Professor Eugen Kogon who, being an opponent of the Nazis, had been imprisoned in Buchenwald. In his book he wrote that Morgen and *SS-Hauptsturmführer* Dr Bernhard Wehner of the *Reichskriminalpolizeiamt* 'had conducted a little experiment in Block 46 in the presence of the camp commander: they had various types of alkaloids added to the soup of four unsuspecting Russian prisoners-of-war. When the men did not die from it, they were strangled immediately afterwards in the crematory.'

The occasion for this experiment was the death of *SS-Hauptscharführer* Köhler. Morgen assumed at the time that Köhler had been poisoned by camp doctor Hoven on orders from Koch to prevent Köhler from testifying against him. To find out what he had been poisoned with, the four Soviet prisoners-of-war were administered toxic substances, supplied by Dr Hoven, to test their reactions. Witnesses declared that the poison had not been added to the soup by Morgen and Wehner, as Kogon asserted, but had been administered to the victims by means of injections by camp doctor Dr Erwin Ding-Schuler. The experiment was conducted in Block 46 in the presence of Morgen and Wehner, who would have been wearing white coats. What exactly had been administered to the guinea pigs is unclear – either the stimulant atropine or the sedative luminal – but the experiment was not fatal. A few days later the human guinea pigs would have had to leave Block 46, and later they were killed somewhere else in the camp.

The charge that Morgen was responsible for administering toxic substances and the killing of four Soviet prisoners-of-war was rejected by the *Landesgericht* in 1961. No evidence was found that Morgen 'had cooperated in any way to the murder of the guinea pigs later on' and there were no indications either that he had 'given the order to conduct the experiment'. While Morgen had no authority over the camp doctor and was not in a position to select inmates for such experiments, it was assumed the order had been given by the RSHA in consultation with the *Reichsarzt-SS*. The possibility that Morgen had requested this experiment or encouraged it was investigated as well. Morgen's former shorthand typist remembered having drafted a letter, dictated by him 'after which an experiment was carried out on various prisoners, sentenced to death, to test the effect of simultaneous administering of sedatives and stimulants'. She did not know whether Morgen had requested this experiment himself or he had been ordered to from higher up, nor did she know to which office the letter had been sent. As the event had occurred seventeen years ago, it could not be excluded that the typist had been in error of the facts or if the letter had been written after the experiments had been carried out. Such a letter from Morgen could not be found, nor could its existence be confirmed by other witnesses than the typist.

The question then remained whether Morgen had actively contributed to the experiment. According to witness Dietzsch, a prisoner in Buchenwald working as a medical orderly and who been present at the experiment, Morgen, Wehner and Ding-Schuler 'had appeared at the experiment, armed with guns and carrying brief cases containing numerous vials'. After they had consulted a chemist's manual for the maximum dosage of the substances involved, they had mutually agreed to administer the maximum dosage seven times over. Morgen denied this and stated that he was only present at the request of Dr Ding-Schuler. This was confirmed by Wehner. The *Landesgericht* judged their version more credible than that of witness Dietzsch as Morgen and Wehner had no medical training, so it made no sense that they would have meddled in the practical conduct of the experiment. The court also indicated that it could not be assumed that a dosage seven times over the maximum was administered, as this would have had serious medical consequences. Morgen's assertion that the inmates had been given a normal dosage of both substances – counteracting each other – was found to be more credible by the *Landesgericht*. Dr Ding-Schuler would have conducted this experiment in this harmless way as he had not seen any sense in the original experiment. The *Landesgericht* concluded there was no proof that Morgen had attended the experiment of Dr Ding-Schuler for anything other than 'comradely reasons' and acquitted him.[5]

As early as 1950, Bernhard Wehner had reported about the experiment with the Russian prisoners of war. His version matched the conclusion of the court for the most part, but according to him it had been Morgen who had asked to conduct the experiment. Arthur Nebe had not granted his permission, and in the end it had been Heinrich Müller who had seen to it that the test could be conducted. Wehner added that the guinea pigs had been sentenced to death but they survived the experience and did not even get sick from it.[6] As he had been involved as well, he had a good reason to shift the blame onto Morgen. It remains vague how it all proceeded exactly, but the fact is Morgen did not subject four inmates to an experiment on his own initiative and it is unlikely he was personally responsible for their deaths later on. After all, he had no authority to decide about life and death of inmates and it is even more unlikely that the man who tried to fight 'illegal murders' now attempted himself, even without permission, to have four prisoners killed. Hence, Kogon's assertion is not credible. It is quite possible that Morgen had submitted a request to his superiors to have this experiment conducted, but evidence is lacking. It is probable that he witnessed the experiment, but as the inmates survived the experiment and were not known to have suffered any serious consequences this was not punishable. He could however also have abstained from attending the experiment out of principle. Appearances are a little against him, as in the case of the Hungarian Jews, but the evidence is so flimsy that the conclusion is justified that during the war Morgen did not commit any crime. Despite the criminal environment he was in, he probably managed to keep his hands clean.

Chapter XXIX

The Devil's Advocate?

L ittle is known about Konrad Morgen's post-war private life, except that he finally married his fiancée Maria Wachter after his release from imprisonment. The couple had wanted to get married during the war, but in 1942 Morgen had not been granted permission from the *Rasse- und Siedlungshauptamt* – the head office of racial and settlements affairs of the SS – as his girlfriend was four and a half years older than he was. Himmler preferred his men to marry young fertile women who could produce sufficient offspring. The couple would not have any children; Maria lost her unborn child during the war when she was injured during an Allied bombardment.[1]

Konrad Morgen passed away on 4 February 1982 at the age of 72.[2] Although he said much about his work during the war as a witness in various trials and in interviews with historians after the war, the lack of clarity about his real motives remain. He presented himself as a lone warrior for justice and asserted he had tried to thwart the Holocaust by prosecuting high-ranking SS men. Historian John Toland concluded he had succeeded in this and attributed a remarkable hero's role to him. But actually much is vague about Morgen's conduct. He remained a member of the SS for the whole war, but during that time he never made any effort to inform the outside world of the atrocities he witnessed. Fighting corruption was the major part of his work; he was to see to it that gold and other valuables of the murdered Jews did not disappear into the lockers of camp guards but into the coffers of the state instead. In this way he contributed to the large-scale plunder by the Nazi government which used the stolen bounty to finance the war.

After the war Morgen never distanced himself from the SS. During the Nuremberg trial he described the SS as a decent organization that had nothing to do with the extermination of the Jews. To substantiate this impossible viewpoint, he did not hesitate to lie, for instance by claiming that Monowitz was an extermination camp not supervised by the SS. He attributed the crimes in the concentration camps to sadistic individuals, but he did not mean the executors of the extermination of the Jews, as they only followed orders from the *Führer* against which protest was impossible. While after the war Morgen was granted the opportunity to help sentence the sadists he could not call to account during the war, he now testified in their favour or claimed he could recall little of their crimes during the war. All told, little remains of the heroism of Konrad Morgen and it seems there are more than enough reasons to consider him a willful servant of the Nazi regime, a devil's advocate.

To determine whether this conclusion is justified it is necessary to distinguish between Morgen's individual motives and his practical achievements. As to the last, it is almost universally acknowledged that thanks to Morgen's personal efforts various camp commanders were arrested and sentenced. The image that Morgen as a judge was single-handedly responsible for the adjudgment of camp commanders needs nuance however. In reality it was not Morgen himself who sentenced the defendants. He conducted the criminal investigation in the camps – the *locus delicti* – along with a team of some fifty other SS judges, and based on the discovered evidence he drafted an indictment. The final verdict however was pronounced by the SS and police courts. Each case was to be approved by a *Gerichtsherr*, someone from the highest echelons of the SS, for instance the head of a *Hauptamt*, an HSSPF, or Heinrich Himmler himself. If Morgen wanted to take a suspect to court with any chance of success, the support of a *Gerichtsherr* was always required.

In the Buchenwald case it was *SS-Obergruppenführer* Waldeck-Pyrmont who as *Gerichtsherr* was the guarantor for the prosecution of Koch and his cronies. Later on, in this and the subsequent cases, it was Himmler himself who granted Morgen permission. This caused Morgen to depend on the double morality of the SS leadership. He was permitted to take judicial action against unreliable and discredited camp commanders such as Karl Koch, but he was never permitted to bring an important executor of the *Endlösung*, for instance Rudolph Höss, to court. Even before Morgen took charge of the investigation into corruption in the concentration camps, as a judge in the General Government he was confronted with this double morality. It was made impossible for him to launch an investigation into Hermann Fegelein and Oskar Dirlewanger who had powerful protectors behind them. In his efforts to prosecute these men he became subjected to the hostility of the SS leadership in the General Government and was degraded and transferred to the *Waffen-SS*.

Despite the establishment of special courts, there was no question of real justice within the SS. All verdicts by SS and police courts against camp commanders had to be approved by Himmler, and more than once he revised a prison sentence to service at the front or to temporary acquittal, for instance in the case against Adam Grünewald, commander of Vught camp. Morgen owes his reputation predominantly to the claim that he was responsible for the death sentence of the sadistic camp commanders Karl Koch and Hermann Florstedt. Apart from the fact that these verdicts had not been pronounced by Morgen himself, and that it is uncertain whether Florstedt was actually sentenced to death and executed, the Nazi regime did not intend to bring about justice out of pity for the victims by prosecuting sadistic commanders.

Himmler's main reason for approving the prosecution of Koch and Florstedt was that they were guilty of exorbitant self-enrichment. The victims' possessions that disappeared into their own pockets should have been transferred to the state. By prosecuting them, an example was set to all others who could not keep their hands off the booty that belonged to the state. Despite all the evidence against him, Koch was not sentenced for killing prisoners of his own accord but for corruption only. Even his wife, Ilse, notorious for her sadism, was acquitted. Sadism and the wanton killing of prisoners was disallowed not for humane reasons but because such transgressions had a negative influence on the economic deployment of prisoners and undermined order and morality among the camp staff. They were transgressions symptomatic of corruption. After all, Koch tortured prisoners, took away their money and murdered them to dispose of them as witnesses to his self-enrichment.

Collectively, camp inmates did not fare much better with the prosecution of camp commanders. By discharging and prosecuting Koch, Florstedt and other sadists, such as Amon Göth of Płaszów camp, prisoners were probably treated less sadistically; all the same they still had to perform exhausting forced labour with the same meagre rations and under the same inhuman living conditions. These conditions were temporarily improved in some camps in 1943 and 1944, but only to improve the productivity of the forced labourers in the war industry and not as a result of Morgen's efforts. His work was mainly advantageous for the concentration camp system, as incompetent commanders who managed their camps ineffectively from an economic point of view were weeded out. Concentration camp staff members who let money and other valuables destined for the state disappear into their own pockets were also dismissed. Morgen's investigations did not lead to the suspension of the extermination of the Jews either. He may have made efforts to bring important executors of the *Endlösung*, such as Rudolph Höss, Christian Wirth and Adolf Eichmann, to court, as he claimed, but he always must have known he would never have succeeded in stopping the extermination of the Jews.

Even if he did succeed in getting Höss, Wirth and Eichmann sentenced, this would not have meant the end of the Holocaust. Though they were experts in murdering, they were not irreplaceable. In 1943 and 1944 the extermination process had evolved in such a way that others could have taken over the role of these men. Moreover, Morgen would have been too late anyway. At the time he launched his investigation into Wirth, almost all Jews in the General Government had been killed, and not long after, the extermination camps at Belzec, Sobibor and Treblinka were closed down. At the time Morgen made efforts to prosecute them, Höss and Eichmann were busily fulfilling their last great task: the extermination of the Hungarian Jews. Within eight weeks, 438,000 of them had been deported to Auschwitz. Shortly after, the *Endlösung* came to a halt, not because of one tiny judge but because the great majority of European Jews had already been murdered and the Red Army was quickly approaching the extermination camps in the East. Himmler continued exterminating the Jews until late in the war and Morgen never obstructed him in any way. The SS chief did attach importance to Morgen's work for removing the bad apples among his men. Eichmann, Wirth and Höss had proved themselves efficient executors of the extermination programme and Himmler would never have allowed them to be put behind bars or have them shot by an SS firing squad, certainly not as long as they could render important services to him.

In conclusion, little is left of the role of hero John Toland has attributed to Morgen. Formal rules to combat sadism and 'illegal murders' lend a semblance of justice to the concentration camp system, but the prisoners could not count on protection from the law. The laws only existed to serve the interests of the state; economic deployment of inmates had to be guaranteed and the possessions taken from deported Jews were destined for the state. The concentration camp was not a part of the *Normenstaat*, bound by laws, but part of the *Massnahmenstaat* in which laws could be ignored or adapted by Himmler who acted on behalf of the *Führer*. Morgen may have seen himself as representative of the *Normenstaat*, but in fact he was more of an instrument of the *Massnahmenstaat*. His work was only a façade which covered the real nature of the system, just like the notices in the dressing rooms reminding the Jews they should remember their wardrobe number while a few minutes later they were gassed. Whatever Morgen did, it was impossible for him to introduce justice into a system which was criminal to the core. In that sense he really was a devil's advocate.

The term devil's advocate implies that Morgen acted as an obliging individual towards the regime with his only goal being to serve it. This is however not the truth either, as Morgen was never a fanatical National Socialist, and he even showed his willingness to row against the National Socialist current. He did so as far back as 1939 when he, as a lay judge in Stettin, protested against the unjustified conviction of a suspect. He did it again in 1942 when, as SS judge in the General Government, he refused to pass a severe sentence on a policeman who had been guilty of 'racial infamy', as demanded by Himmler. In both cases this caused his discharge; in the second he was even transferred to a penal unit, which means he barely escaped imprisonment in a concentration camp.

In the course of his investigations in the camps, Morgen went against the interests of high SS leaders more than once, especially Oswald Pohl who did everything in his power to protect his protégées against Morgen's attempts to take them to court. Morgen could have taken the easy way out by limiting himself to small transgressions by lower-ranking guards, but he also set his sights on higher-ranking officers who were feared by their prisoners and subordinates alike. He and his colleagues were often treated in a hostile fashion and their work was not without risks, as exemplified by the fact that in Buchenwald a guard was probably poisoned by his colleagues to dispose of him as a witness. Morgen not only displayed guts by entering the concentration camps and taking judicial steps against the most notorious camp commanders, but from the report he wrote on occasion of the Buchenwald case it appears he was genuinely indignant about Koch's sadism and his crimes and the gruesome circumstances in which his prisoners were forced to live.

Morgen could have done little or nothing to improve these conditions, but that does not mean he did not try. He must have known he could not change this criminal system, but prosecuting the most sadistic camp officers was the least he could do. He knew he could not mean anything to the Jews, but it is possible that he, through his investigations in the camps, really thought he could improve the system from within, hoping to contribute in his way to the living conditions of the inmates. It is to his advantage that he was probably never guilty of crimes himself, despite his frequent presence when and where the most serious crimes were committed. He did keep his hands off the many valuables he discovered in the camps.

In a certain sense, it seems Morgen acted out of pity for the victims, but probably ambition was a motive of no less importance. The same ambition had triggered a conflict with Karl Julius Speck in 1938 with whom he had wanted to fight a duel to defend his honour. During the war he wanted to portray himself as a righteous judge, and that was the image he wanted to preserve after the war. To acquit himself he claimed to have joined the SS involuntarily, and during the Nuremberg trial he tried to present the SS as a decent organization. After everything he had seen in the concentration and extermination camps though, he knew better. He hid behind the fact that at the time, the murder of the Jews was a legal task, ordered by the government. During the Auschwitz trial his explanation contributed to the semblance of legitimacy that was attributed to the murder programme. In his testimonies, the ambitious lawyer emerges frequently – and not the warrior for humanity he claimed to have been during the war. As for many of his well-educated countrymen, the Nazi regime offered him the opportunity of a fine judicial career within the SS. Zealous as he was, he tried to get various camp commanders and important officers behind bars, which earned him the reputation after the war of having been a righteous crime fighter.

Although Morgen's intentions were probably well-meant in principle and he was not a corrupt or bloodthirsty villain, he was after all a servant of the law in the wrong place and in the wrong time. Under these circumstances a hero's role could not be attributed to him. Instead of bringing justice, he was sucked into the criminal system. Diligent in his work, he contributed to the prevention of corruption, benefitting the coffers of the state. Contributing to the crimes of the Third Reich was not his goal though, he served the law and tried – against his better judgment – to introduce a little justice into a criminal and almost lawless society. That was an impossible task which no one, including Konrad Morgen, could ever hope to achieve.

Notes

Chapter I
1. Smith, L., *Vergeten stemmen van de Holocaust*, pp. 322–3.
2. Ibid., p. 323.

Chapter II
1. Hitler is often – incorrectly – thought of as the spiritual father of the Autobahn. Before he came to power though, developments and plans already existed to connect German cities with highways.
2. IMT Nuremberg, Hearing Konrad Morgen, 07-08-1946; Denazification Ludwigsburg 1948, EL 90313, Bü2196, Landesarchiv Baden-Württemberg; Personnel file Konrad Morgen, US National Archives.
3. Recorded interview with John Toland, 25-10-1971, Franklin D. Roosevelt Library.
4. Holmes, R., *De wereld in oorlog*, p. 47.
5. Personnel file Konrad Morgen, US National Archives.
6. Denazification Ludwigsburg 1948.
7. Bundesarchiv, 'Ministerbesprechung vom 12. September 1932', on: www.bundesarchiv.de/aktenreichskanzlei/1919-1933/1011/vpa/vpa2p/kap1_1/kap2_3/para3_5.html.
8. Holmes, R., p. 48.
9. Denazification Ludwigsburg 1948.
10. Personnel file Konrad Morgen, US National Archives.
11. Denazification Ludwigsburg 1948.
12. Kershaw, I., *Hitler: Hoogmoed 1889–1936*, p. 680.
13. Holmes, R., p. 53.
14. Denazification Ludwigsburg 1948.
15. Recorded interview with John Toland.
16. Holmes, R., *De wereld in oorlog*, p. 49.
17. Ibid., p. 54.

Chapter III
1. IMT Nuremberg, Hearing Konrad Morgen, 07-08-1946.
2. Denazification Ludwigsburg 1948, EL 90313, Bü2196, Landesarchiv Baden-Württemberg.
3. Morgen, K., *Kriegspropaganda und Kriegsverhütung*, pp. 16–17.
4. Ibid., p. 106.
5. Ibid., pp. 108–9.
6. E-mail from Randall Bytwerk to author, 29-01-2010.
7. Koszyk, K., *Pressepolitik und Propaganda im Ersten Weltkrieg*, p. 467.
8. The real number of German deaths at Verdun is estimated at 143,000.
9. Recorded interview with John Toland, 25-10-1971, Franklin D. Roosevelt Library.
10. Personnel file Konrad Morgen, US National Archives.

11. Longerich, P., *Heinrich Himmler*, p. 313.
12. Personnel file Konrad Morgen.
13. Denazification Ludwigsburg 1948.
14. Ibid.

Chapter IV
1. Denazification Ludwigsburg 1948, EL 90313, Bü2196, Landesarchiv Baden-Württemberg.
2. Evans, R.J., *Het Derde Rijk: Dictatuur*, pp. 55–6.
3. Kershaw, I., *Hitler: Hoogmoed 1889–1936*, p. 670; Evans, R.J, *Het Derde Rijk: Dictatuur*, p. 51.
4. Wachsmann, N., *KL: een geschiedenis van de naziconcentratiekampen*, p. 53.
5. Evans, R.J., *Het Derde Rijk: Dictatuur*, p. 92.
6. Read, A., *Discipelen van de Duivel*, p. 325; Evans, R.J., *Het Derde Rijk: Dictatuur*, p. 92; Hilmar Wäckerle was not sentenced: during the war he served in the *Waffen-SS*, including the battle of the Grebbeberg.
7. Knopp, G., *Hitlers moordenaars*, p. 47.

Chapter V
1. Evans, R.J., *Het Derde Rijk: Oorlog*, p. 38.
2. 'Hitler and Murders in Poland 1939–1940', on: forum.axishistory.com/viewtopic.php?f=6&t=24138&start=15.
3. Weingartner, J.J., 'Law and Justice in the Nazi SS: The Case of Konrad Morgen', *Central European History*, vol. 16, nr. 3, September 1983, pp. 276–82.
4. Auschwitz trial Frankfurt, statement Konrad Morgen, 09-03-1964.
5. Weingartner, J.J., pp. 276–82.
6. Ibid., p. 280.
7. Ibid., p. 280.
8. Ibid., p. 282.
9. Longerich, P., *Heinrich Himmler*, p. 313.
10. Speech by Heinrich Himmler in Posen, 04-10-1943, on: www.tracesofwar.nl/articles/1236/Toespraak-Himmler-in-Poznan-04-10-1943.htm.

Chapter VI
1. Personnel file Konrad Morgen, US National Archives.
2. Denazification Ludwigsburg 1948, EL 90313, Bü2196, Landesarchiv Baden-Württemberg.
3. Ibid.
4. Personnel file Georg von Sauberzweig, on: forum.axishistory.com/viewtopic.php?f=38&t=39441; Weingartner, J.J., 'Law and Justice in the Nazi SS: The Case of Konrad Morgen', *Central European History*, vol. 16, nr. 3, September 1983, p. 283.
5. Weingartner, J.J., pp. 283–5.
6. Denazification Ludwigsburg 1948, EL 90313, Bü2196, Landesarchiv Baden-Württemberg.
7. Breitman, R., *Heinrich Himmler, de architect van de Holocaust*, pp. 321–2.
8. Ibid., p. 180.
9. Weingartner, J.J., p. 285; Pauer-Studer, H. & Velleman, J.D., *Konrad Morgen: The Conscience of a Nazi Judge*, pp. 36–7.
10. Hilberg, R., *De vernietiging van de Europese Joden*, p. 1189.
11. An expansive discussion on the question of whether or not the Nazis produced soap from the bodies of murdered Jews can be found on: www.nizkor.org

12. Weingartner, J.J., pp. 285–6.
13. Ibid., p. 286.
14. Ibid., pp. 286–7; Denazification Ludwigsburg 1948, EL 90313, Bü2196, Landesarchiv Baden-Württemberg.
15. Pauer-Studer, H. & Velleman, J.D., p. 19.
16. Denazification Ludwigsburg 1948.
17. Pauer-Studer, H. & Velleman, J.D., p. 21.
18. Weingartner, J.J., p. 287.
19. Pauer-Studer, H. & Velleman, J.D., p. 41; from October 1939 onwards, Wilhelm Koppe was *Höhere SS- und Polizeiführer* in the Wartheland region and plenipotentiary of the *Reichskommissar für die Festigung des Deutschen Volkstums*. In November 1943 he succeeded Friedrich Krüger as HSSPF in the General Government.
20. Pauer-Studer, H. & Velleman, J.D., p. 90.

Chapter VII

1. Denazification Ludwigsburg 1948, EL 90313, Bü2196, Landesarchiv Baden-Württemberg.
2. Holmes, R., *De wereld in oorlog*, p. 354.
3. Friedländer, S., *Nazi-Duitsland en de Joden: de jaren van vernietiging*, p. 345–6.
4. Höhne, H., *Het zwarte korps onder de doodskop*, p. 382.
5. Ibid., p. 375.
6. Ibid., pp. 375–6.

Chapter VIII

1. Rozett, R. & Spector, S., *Encyclopedie van de Holocaust*, p. 155.
2. Hilberg, R., *De vernietiging van de Europese Joden*, pp. 1118–9; Hilberg substantiates his claim on a testimony dated 11 July 1946 by Dr Werner Paulmann, deputy judge and later on chief of the *SS- und Polizeigerichthof* in Kassel.
3. Weingartner, J.J., 'Law and Justice in the Nazi SS: The Case of Konrad Morgen', *Central European History*, vol. 16, nr. 3, September 1983, p. 288.
4. Wehner, B., 'Das Spiel ist Aus - Arthur Nebe Glanz und Elend der Deutschen Kriminalpolizei', *Der Spiegel*, nr. 8, 23-02-1950.
5. Morgen, K., *Wesentliches Ermittlungsergebnis. Der Korruptionskomplex A. SS-Standartenfuehrer Koch*, Harvard Law School Library, p. 32.
6. Ibid., p. 33–4.
7. Holmes, R., *De wereld in oorlog*, p. 354.
8. IMT Nuremberg, hearing Konrad Morgen, 07-08-1946.
9. Wehner, B.
10. Morgen, K., p. 52.
11. Ibid., p. 45.
12. Ibid., p. 59.
13. Ibid., p. 60.
14. Pauer-Studer, H. & Velleman, J.D., *Konrad Morgen: The Conscience of a Nazi Judge*, p.58.
15. 'West Germany: The Monster', *Time Magazine*, 14-07-1958, on: www.time.com/magazine/
16. Morgen, K., p. 68.
17. Denazification Ludwigsburg 1948, EL 90313, Bü2196, Landesarchiv Baden-Württemberg.
18. Ibid.

Chapter IX

1. Wehner, B., 'Das Spiel ist Aus - Arthur Nebe Glanz und Elend der deutschen Kriminalpolizei', *Der Spiegel*, nr. 8, 23-02-1950; Pauer-Studer, H. & Velleman, J.D., *Konrad Morgen: The Conscience of a Nazi Judge*, p. 63.
2. Personnel file Konrad Morgen, US National Archives.
3. Weingartner, J.J., 'Law and Justice in the Nazi SS: The Case of Konrad Morgen', *Central European History*, vol. 16, nr. 3, September 1983, p. 290–2.
4. Ibid., p. 293; Klee, p. 324.
5. Stein, H., *Buchenwald concentration camp*, p.58; Klee, E., *Das Personenlexikon zum Dritten Reich*, p. 272; Stein, *Buchenwald concentration camp*, p. 307.
6. Stein, H., p.308; 'West Germany: The Monster', *Time Magazine*, 14-07-1958, on: www.time.com/magazine; Klee, E., *Das Personenlexikon zum Dritten Reich*, p. 586.
7. Rozett, R. & Spector, S., *Encyclopedie van de Holocaust*, p. 315–16.
8. Morgen, K., *Wesentliches Ermittlungsergebnis. Der Korruptionskomplex A. SS-Standartenfuehrer Koch*, Harvard Law School Library, p. 45.
9. Hilberg, R., *De vernietiging van de Europese Joden*, pp. 1119–20.
10. Ibid., p. 1119; Klee, E., *Das Personenlexikon zum Dritten Reich*, p. 215.

Chapter X

1. Personnel file Hermann Florstedt, Das Bundesarchiv.
2. Lindner, P., 'Überlebte Hermann Florstedt den Zweiten Weltkrieg?', *Zeitschrift für Heimatforschung*, 10, 2001, p. 81.
3. Ibid., p. 75.
4. Ibid., p. 77.

Chapter XI

1. Holmes, R., *De wereld in oorlog*, p. 353.
2. Weingartner, J.J., 'Law and Justice in the Nazi SS: The Case of Konrad Morgen', *Central European History*, vol. 16, nr. 3, September 1983, p. 289.
3. IMT Nuremberg, hearing Konrad Morgen, 07-08-1946.
4. Recorded interview with John Toland, 25-10-1971, Franklin D. Roosevelt Library; John Toland incorrectly calls him the 'blood hound judge' in his book.
5. IMT Nuremberg, hearing Konrad Morgen, 07-08-1946.
6. Höhne, H., *Het zwarte korps onder de doodskop*, p. 379.
7. Allen, M.T., *The Business of Genocide*, p. 178
8. Klee, E., *Das Personenlexikon zum Dritten Reich*, p. 349.
9. MacLean, F.L., *The Camp Men*, p. 140.
10. Longerich, P., *Heinrich Himmler*, p. 326.
11. Allen, M.T., *The Business of Genocide*, p. 178
12. MacLean, F.L., p. 140.
13. Höhne, H., p. 379.
14. Nazi Crimes on Trial, on: www1.jur.uva.nl/junsv; MacLean, F.L. *The Camp Men*, p. 177; Klee, E., *Das Personenlexikon zum Dritten Reich*, p. 463.
15. Höhne, H., *Het zwarte korps onder de doodskop* p. 379.
16. MacLean, F.L. p. 148; Klee, E., *Das Personenlexikon zum Dritten Reich* , p. 381.
17. Yerger, M.C., *Allgemeine-SS*, p. 189.
18. Klee, E., *Das Personenlexikon zum Dritten Reich*, p. 381.
19. Hilberg, R., *De vernietiging van de Europese Joden*, pp. 1119–20.
20. Höhne, H., p. 378.
21. Yerger, M.C., *Allgemeine-SS*, p. 189; Klee, E., *Das Personenlexikon zum Dritten Reich*, p. 381.

Chapter XII

1. Personnel file Adam Grünewald, Das Bundesarchiv.
2. Klee, E., *Das Personenlexikon zum Dritten Reich*, p. 91: in October 1943 Chmielewski was relieved of his post and arrested. In 1944 an SS court sentenced him to 15 years imprisonment. Himmler quashed the verdict though. On 11 April 1961 the *Landesgericht* Ansbach sentenced him to life imprisonment for crimes committed in Gusen camp.
3. Uijland, M. & Tijenk, C., *Eindpunt of tussenstation/Gids Nationaal Monument Kamp Vught*, p. 9.
4. Personnel file Adam Grünewald.
5. Olink, H., *Vrouwen van Vught*, pp. 38, 40, 42, 48, 49.
6. Uijland, M. & Tijenk, C., *Eindpunt of tussenstation/Gids Nationaal Monument Kamp Vught*.
7. Personnel file Adam Grünewald.
8. Olink, H., pp. 53, 59–61, 71.
9. Personnel file Adam Grünewald.
10. Olink, H., p. 72.
11. Olink, H., pp. 66–73.
12. IMT Nuremberg, hearing Konrad Morgen, 08-08-1946.
13. Personnel file Adam Grünewald.
14. Ibid.; Klee, E., *Das Personenlexikon zum Dritten Reich*, p. 675.
15. Personnel file Adam Grünewald; Klee, E., *Das Personenlexikon zum Dritten Reich*, p. 206; MacLean, F.L., *The Camp Men*, p. 93

Chapter XIII

1. IMT Nuremberg, hearing Konrad Morgen, 07-08-1946.
2. Sereny, G., *De duisternis tegemoet*, p. 125.
3. Ibid., p. 122.
4. Arad, Y., *Belzec, Sobibor, Treblinka*, p. 162.
5. Ibid., pp. 153, 160–1, 165, 177.
6. Holocaust Education & Archive Research Team, 'Christian Wirth: Dealer in Death', on: www.holocaustresearchproject.org/ar/wirth.html
7. Schelvis, J., *Ooggetuigen van Sobibor*, p. 10.
8. Arad, Y., p. 369.
9. Ibid., p. 366.
10. Office of the United States Chief of Counsel For Prosecution of Axis Criminality, *International Military Trials*, Supplement B, pp. 1309–11.
11. During my investigation into Konrad Morgen, I had e-mail contact with David Luck, author of the essay 'Use and abuse of Holocaust Documents: Reitlinger and "How many?"' (in *Jewish Social Studies*, vol. 41, nr. 2, 1979, pp. 95–122). In this essay he mentions the words attributed to Morgen about Poniatowa during the hearing of Ernst Kaltenbrunner. In 1972, Luck had a telephone conversation with Konrad Morgen, so he claimed in an e-mail to me. According to him, Morgen considered the executions in Poniatowa 'both necessary and legal according to the law, regarding the fact that these Jews ... had ties with (communist) partisans operating in the hinterland of the camps ... and stored clothing, munitions and explosives.' Walter Többens, the owner of the clothing factory, so David Luck claims, reportedly would have appeared during the executions and had attempted to stop the killing. Thereupon, Morgen would have locked him up in the camp kitchen for the duration of the operation. What Luck writes here definitely does not paint a favourable

picture of Morgen, but I have abstained from using this information. David Luck has neither been able to submit a transcript of this telephone conversation nor any other publication describing or substantiating his claim. In view of the fact that none of the claims can be verified and in addition the fact that this phone conversation took place almost forty years ago, I think this information is not sufficiently dependable. By the way, it is correct that weapons were collected by inmates of Poniatowa who had established a resistance movement in the camp. When the mass execution had almost finished, members of the underground movement opened fire on the guards. They put the barracks, which held the last remaining Jews, to the torch, causing all (the Jews) to die (source: *Arad, Y., Belzec, Sobibor, Treblinka*, p. 367).

12. IMT Nuremberg, hearing Konrad Morgen, 07-08-1946.
13. IMT Nuremberg, hearing Konrad Morgen, 08-08-1946.
14. IMT Nuremberg, hearing Konrad Morgen, 07-08-1946.
15. Maclean, F.L., *The Camp Men*, p. 259.

Chapter XIV

1. Jeffreys, D., *Het kartel van de hel*, pp. 363, 430.
2. Levi, P., *Is dit een mens*, pp. 84–5.
3. Rees, L., *Auschwitz*, p. 182.
4. Van Pelt, R.J. & Dwork, D., *Auschwitz*, pp. 292–3.
5. Rozett, R. & Spector, S., *Encyclopedie van de Holocaust*, p. 121.
6. Van Pelt, R.J. & Dwork, D., *Auschwitz*, p. 343.
7. Auschwitz trial Frankfurt, testimony Konrad Morgen, 09-03-1964.
8. IMT Nuremberg, hearing Konrad Morgen, 08-08-1946.
9. Holmes, R., *De wereld in oorlog*, pp. 355–6.

Chapter XV

1. Personnel file Konrad Morgen, US National Archives.
2. Holmes, R., *De wereld in oorlog*, p. 356.
3. Auschwitz trial Frankfurt, testimony Konrad Morgen, 09-03-1964.
4. Holmes, R., *De wereld in oorlog*, p. 356.
5. Auschwitz trial Frankfurt, testimony Konrad Morgen, 09-03-1964.
6. Höss, R., *Commandant van Auschwitz*, p. 59.
7. Ibid., pp. 77–8.
8. Ibid., p. 112.
9. Ibid., pp. 108–10.
10. Ibid., p. 157.
11. Knopp, G., *Hitlers moordenaars*, p. 184.
12. Auschwitz trial Frankfurt, testimony Konrad Morgen, 09-03-1964.

Chapter XVI

1. Vrba, R., *Ik ontsnapte uit Auschwitz*, p. 113.
2. Ibid., p. 159.
3. Ibid., p. 165.
4. Ibid., p. 164.
5. Ibid., p. 186.
6. Rees, L., *Auschwitz*, pp. 168–9.
7. Höss, R., *Commandant van Auschwitz*, p. 159.
8. United States Holocaust Museum, 'Auschwitz through the lens of the SS: Photos of Nazi leadership at the camp', on www.ushmm.org

9. Friedländer, S., *Nazi-Duitsland en de Joden: de jaren van vernietiging*, pp. 600–1, 604.
10. Vrba, R., pp. 209–10.
11. The Auschwitz-Birkenau State Museum, 'Reminiscences of Perry Broad', *KL Auschwitz seen by the SS*, p. 145.
12. Höss, R., pp. 197–8.

Chapter XVII
1. The Auschwitz-Birkenau State Museum, 'Reminiscences of Perry Broad', *KL Auschwitz seen by the SS*, p. 145; Klee, E., *Das Personenlexikon zum Dritten Reich*, p. 119.
2. Langbein, H., *Menschen in Auschwitz*, p. 300.
3. Rees, L., *Auschwitz*, pp. 200–1.
4. Langbein, H., p. 299.
5. Wittmann, R., *Beyond justice*, p. 165.
6. Ibid., pp. 90–1.
7. The Auschwitz-Birkenau State Museum, *KL Auschwitz as seen by the SS*, p. 230.
8. The Auschwitz-Birkenau State Museum, 'Reminiscences of Perry Broad', *KL Auschwitz seen by the SS*, p. 108.
9. Langbein, H., *Menschen in Auschwitz*, p. 330.
10. IMT Nuremberg, hearing Konrad Morgen, 08-08-1946.
11. Wittmann, R., *Beyond justice*, p. 165.
12. Langbein, H., p. 331.
13. Wittmann, R., pp. 166–7.
14. Langbein, H., pp. 331–2.
15. Ibid., p. 332; Klee, E., *Das Personenlexikon zum Dritten Reich*, p. 195.
16. Langbein, H., pp. 301, 331.
17. *KL Auschwitz as seen by the SS*, p. 228, 250–1; Klee, E., *Das Personenlexikon zum Dritten Reich*, pp. 21, 572.

Chapter XVIII
1. Hilberg, R., *De vernietiging van de Europese Joden*, p. 1120.
2. E-mail from Sandra Webers of the International Tracing Service of the Red Cross, 28-04-2010.
3. Hearing Eleonore Hodys by Konrad Morgen, autumn 1944, The Auschwitz-Birkenau State Museum.
4. Holmes, R., *De wereld in oorlog*, p. 358.
5. Hearing Eleonore Hodys by Konrad Morgen.
6. Langbein, H., Menschen *in Auschwitz*, p. 413.
7. IMT Nuremberg, hearing Günter Reinecke, 07-08-1946.
8. Hearing Eleonore Hodys by Konrad Morgen.
9. Sonnenfeldt, R, *Witness to Nuremberg*, p. 68.
10. E-mail from Sandra Webers of the International Tracing Service of the Red Cross, 28-04-2010.

Chapter XIX
1. Höhne, H., *Het zwarte korps onder de doodskop*, p. 379.
2. Wittmann, R., *Beyond justice*, p. 1120.
3. Klee, E., *Das Personenlexikon zum Dritten Reich*, p. 448; Axis History Forum.
4. IMT Nuremberg, hearing Konrad Morgen, 08-08-1946.

5. Langbein, H., *Menschen in Auschwitz*, p. 300.
6. Wittmann, R., pp. 165–6.
7. Hilberg, R., *De vernietiging van de Europese Joden*, p. 1120.
8. Höhne, H., *Het zwarte korps onder de doodskop*, p. 379.
9. IMT Nuremberg, hearing Günter Reinecke, 07-08-1946.
10. Personnel file Konrad Morgen, The National Archieves.
11. The Auschwitz-Birkenau State Museum, *KL Auschwitz as seen by the SS*, p. 239; Klee, E., *Das Personenlexikon zum Dritten Reich*, p. 263.
12. Höss, R., *Commandant van Auschwitz*, p. 243.
13. Goldensohn, L., *Neurenberggesprekken*, p. 344.
14. Rees, L., *Auschwitz*, p. 232; Klee, E., *Das Personenlexikon zum Dritten Reich*, p. 263.
15. IMT Nuremberg, hearing Günter Reinecke, 07-08-1946.
16. Rozett, R. & Spector, S., *Encyclopedie van de Holocaust*, p. 122.

Chapter XX
1. Crowe, D.M., *Oskar Schindler*, pp. 243–9, 251–5.
2. Rozett, R. & Spector, S., *Encyclopedie van de Holocaust*, pp. 365–6.
3. Crowe, D.M., p. 260.
4. The United Nations War Crimes Commission, Case No. 37, Trial of Hauptsturmführer Amon Leopold Göth, Volume VII, London, HMSO, 1948.
5. Smith, L., *Vergeten stemmen van de Holocaust*, pp. 206–8.
6. Trial of Hauptsturmführer Amon Leopold Göth.
7. Crowe, D.M., p. 374.
8. Trial of Hauptsturmführer Amon Leopold Göth.
9. Crowe, D.M., pp. 318, 385.
10. IMT Nuremberg, hearing Konrad Morgen, 07-08-1946.
11. Crowe, D.M., *Oskar Schindler*, pp. 385–6.
12. Ibid., p. 386.
13. Ibid., p. 388.
14. Ibid., p. 391.
15. Ibid., pp. 389–91.
16. Ibid., pp. 387,395.
17. Ibid., p. 476.
18. Keneally, T., *Schindlers List*, pp. 407–8.

Chapter XXI
1. Klee, E., *Das Personenlexikon zum Dritten Reich*, p. 416; Weingartner, J.J., 'Law and Justice in the Nazi SS: The Case of Konrad Morgen', *Central European History*, vol. 16, nr. 3, September 1983, p. 293; Denazification Ludwigsburg 1948, EL 90313, Bü2196, Landesarchiv Baden-Württemberg.
2. Holmes, R., *De wereld in oorlog*, p. 632; Recorded interview with John Toland, 25-10-1971, Franklin D. Roosevelt Library.
3. Pauer-Studer, H. & Velleman, J.D., *Konrad Morgen: The Conscience of a Nazi Judge*, p. 115.
4. Recorded interview with John Toland, 25-10-1971, Franklin D. Roosevelt Library.
5. Holmes, R., p. 632.
6. IMT Nuremberg, hearing Konrad Morgen, 08-08-1946.
7. Ibid.; Seventh Army Interrogation Center, Preliminary Interrogation Report, 01.10-1945, US National Archives.

8. Preliminary Interrogation Report, 01.10-1945.
9. Marcuse, H., *Legacies of Dachau*, p. 98.
10. IMT Nuremberg, hearing Konrad Morgen, 08-08-1946.
11. Klee, E., *Das Personenlexikon zum Dritten Reich*, p. 215; Stiftung Gedenkstätten Buchenwald und Mittelbau-Dora, on: www.buchenwald.de

Chapter XXII

1. Wistrich, R.S., *Who's who in Nazi Germany*, p. 143.
2. Morgen, K., *Wesentliches Ermittlungsergebnis. Der Korruptionskomplex A. SS-Standartenfuehrer Koch*, Harvard Law School Library, p. 50.
3. 'Ilse Koch Lady mit Lampenschirm', *Der Spiegel*, nr. 7, 16.02.1950.
4. Toland, J., *Adolf Hitler*, p. 846.
5. Holmes, R., *De Wereld in oorlog*, p. 637.
6. Knopp, G., *Hitlers moordenaars*, p. 236.
7. Subcommittee of the Committee on Armed Services U.S. Senate, Malmedy Massacre Investigation, 13-10-1949, US National Archives.
8. Griffith, R., *The Politics of Fear: Joseph R. McCarthy and the Senate*, p. 22.
9. Malmedy Massacre Investigation.
10. Knopp, G., *Hitlers moordenaars*, p. 236.
11. 'Ilse Koch Lady mit Lampenschirm'.
12. Ibid.
13. Stein, H., 'Stimmt es, dass die SS im KZ Buchenwald Lampenschirme aus Menschenhaut anfertigen ließ?' on: www.buchenwald.de/index.php?p= nachgefragt_lampenschirme; Recorded interview with John Toland, 25-10-1971, Franklin D. Roosevelt Library.
14. 'Ilse Koch Lady mit Lampenschirm'.
15. Snyder, L.L., *Encyclopedia of the Third Reich*, p. 198.
16. 'Ilse Koch Lady mit Lampenschirm'.
17. Snyder, L.L., p. 198.

Chapter XXIII

1. IMT Nuremberg, hearing Konrad Morgen, 07-08-1946.
2. Recorded interview with John Toland, 25-10-1971, Franklin D. Roosevelt Library.
3. IMT Nuremberg, hearing Konrad Morgen, 08-08-1946.
4. Recorded interview with John Toland.
5. IMT Nuremberg, hearing Konrad Morgen, 07-08-1946.
6. Klee, E., *Das Personenlexikon zum Dritten Reich*, p. 680.
7. IMT Nuremberg, hearing Konrad Morgen, 08-08-1946.
8. Ibid.
9. Rees, L., *Auschwitz*, pp. 204–7.
10. Rozett, R. & Spector, S., *Encyclopedie van de Holocaust*, p. 319, 340, 432.
11. Included are the nameless victims who had been brought in from the East in 1945 and the inmates who perished in April 1945 during the death marches from Buchenwald. The number of deaths in Buchenwald from 1937 to 31 March 1945, as recorded by the SS, stands at 33,462 (14%).
12. Stein, H., *Buchenwald concentration camp 1937–1945*, p. 253. The figures only pertain to male inmates.
13. Denazification Ludwigsburg 1948, EL 90313, Bü2196, Landesarchiv Baden-Württemberg.
14. Evans, R.J., *Het Derde Rijk: Oorlog*, p. 399.

15. Stein, H., p. 253.
16. Tissier, T. le, *The Third Reich Then and Now*, p. 321.
17. Stiftung Gedenkstätten Buchenwald und Mittelbau-Dora, on: www.buchenwald.de/english/index.php?p=Alias_139
18. IMT Nuremberg, hearing Konrad Morgen, 08-08-1946.
19. KZ-Gedenkstätte Dachau, on: www.kz-gedenkstaette-dachau.de/index2.html

Chapter XXIV
1. In 2013 Johannes Tuchel, manager of the German Resistance Memorial Centre in Berlin, stated in *Das Bild* that Müller's body had been buried in 1945 in a mass grave in the Jewish cemetery of Berlin-Mitte. Remains have never been found though.
2. IMT Nuremberg, hearing Konrad Morgen, 08-08-1946.
3. Ibid.
4. Friedlander, H., *The Origins of Nazi Genocide: From Euthanasia to the Final Solution*, pp. 149–50.
5. Holmes, R., *De wereld in oorlog*, p. 363–4.
6. Toland, J., *Adolf Hitler*, p. 845.
7. Ibid., p. 904.
8. Recorded interview with John Toland, 25-10-1971, Franklin D. Roosevelt Library.
9. Rees, L., *Auschwitz*, p. 268.

Chapter XXV
1. Goldensohn, L., *Neurenberggesprekken*, pp. 427, 429, 430–1.
2. Arad, Y., *Belzec, Sobibor, Treblinka*, p. 109.
3. Goldensohn, L., p. 432–3, 436.
4. Trials of War Criminals before the Nuremberg Military Tribunals, Volume V, 'The Pohl Case', p. 200.
5. Ibid., pp. 273–4.
6. Ibid., pp. 895–6.
7. Ibid., p. 934.
8. IMT Nuremberg, hearing Günter Reinecke, 07-08-1946.
9. Bloxham, D., *Genocide on Trial*, pp. 123–4.
10. Marcuse, H., *Legacies of Dachau: the uses and abuses of a concentration camp*, 1933–2001, p. 254.
11. 'The Pohl Case', p. 1077.
12. Ibid., pp. 983–4, 989.
13. Ibid., p. 1062.
14. United States Holocaust Museum, 'Subsequent Nuremberg Proceedings, Case #4, The Pohl Case', on: www.ushmm.org/wlc/en/article.php?ModuleId=10007075; Harvard Law School Library, 'Pohl Case Overview', on: Nuremberg.law.harvard.edu

Chapter XXVI
1. Denazification Ludwigsburg 1948, EL 90313, Bü2196, Landesarchiv Baden-Württemberg.
2. Denazification Nordwürttemburg 1950, EL 90313, Bü2196, Landesarchiv Baden-Württemberg.

Chapter XXVII
1. E-mail from the Rechtsanwaltskammer Frankfurt am Main, 4-12-2009.
2. This was the first of three Auschwitz trials that took place in the sixties in Frankfurt am Main. The other two were held in 1965/6 and 1967/8 against respectively three

members of the SS and against two *Funktionshäftlinge* (inmates who had been in charge of other inmates).

3. Jewish Virtual Library, 'Auschwitz Trial', on: www.jewishvirtuallibrary.org
4. Pendas, D.O., *The Frankfurt Auschwitz trial*, 1963–1965, p. 2.
5. Fritz Bauer Institut, 'Der Auschwitz-Prozess', on: www.saalbau.com/auschwitz-prozess
6. Wittmann, R., *Beyond justice*, p. 163.
7. Ibid., pp. 167–9.
8. Ibid., pp. 170–1.
9. Ibid., pp. 172–3.
10. Pendas, D.O., pp. 291, 297.
11. Fritz Bauer Institut.
12. Wittmann, R., pp. 271–2.
13. Hinke, B., 'Demjanjuk vijf jaar de cel in voor wandaden in kamp Sobibor', *NRC*, 12-05-2011, on: www.nrc.nl/nieuws/2011/05/12/demjanjuk-vijf-jaar-de-cel-in-voor-wandaden-in-kamp-sobibor/

Chapter XXVIII
1. Ermittlungsverfahren gegen Konrad Morgen, 07-07-1955, Abt./Nr. 461/32808, Hessisches Hauptstaatsarchiv.
2. Ermittlungsverfahren gegen Konrad Morgen, 06-03-1972, Abt./Nr. 461/31502, Hessisches Hauptstaatsarchiv.
3. Pauer-Studer, H. & Velleman, J.D., *Konrad Morgen: The Conscience of a Nazi Judge*, p. 104.
4. IMT Nuremberg, hearing Konrad Morgen, 08-08-1946.
5. Ermittlungsverfahren gegen Konrad Morgen, 29-03-1961, Abt./Nr. 461/303942, Hessisches Hauptstaatsarchiv.
6. Wehner, B., 'Das Spiel ist Aus - Arthur Nebe Glanz und Elend der deutschen Kriminalpolizei', *Der Spiegel*, nr. 8, 23-02-1950.

Chapter XXIX
1. Pauer-Studer, H. & Velleman, J.D., *Konrad Morgen: The Conscience of a Nazi Judge*, p. 118.
2. Death certificate Konrad Morgen, Standesamt Stadt Frankfurt am Main.

Acknowledgements

I thank Gerd van der Auwera of STIWOT (Foundation for information on World War Two) for having edited the original Dutch text and his numerous useful observations. Johan van den Ende, who intends to write a novel about Konrad Morgen himself, provided me with useful feedback, as did Wesley Dankers of STIWOT.

I also extend my gratitude to Richard Doetkott, professor in the faculty of communication of Chapman University in California. Fascinated by Konrad Morgen like myself, he has assisted me in collecting sources from the United States. Sadly he did not live to see the publication of this book, as he unexpectedly died from a heart attack in December 2011.

I have also been assisted by Randall Bytwerk, professor of communication at Calvin College in Grand Rapids, Michigan. Thanks also to Wojciech Płosa of the Auschwitz-Birkenau State Museum and Sandra Webers of the Red Cross International Tracing Service at Bad Arolsen for their information.

Further thanks are due to Arnold Palthe, who did a great job translating this book into English. And also my gratitude to Henry Wilson, Barnaby Blacker, Matthew Jones and other staff members of Pen & Sword Books for their collaboration in publishing this book in English.

Glossary

Aktion Reinhard	Code name for the extermination of the Jews from the General Government in the extermination camps at Belzec, Sobibor and Treblinka.
Allgemeine-SS	Civilian branch of the SS.
Blockälteste	Inmate of a concentration camp appointed as leader of the inmates in a barracks.
Blockführer	Member of the camp staff of the SS, charged with supervision of prisoners from one or more barracks.
Einsatzgruppen	Death squads consisting of members of the *Sicherheitspolizei*, SD, *Ordnungspolizei* and *Waffen-SS*, deployed behind the front during the German invasion of Poland and the Soviet Union to execute political opponents, partisans, Jews and gypsies.
Endlösung	Euphemistic Nazi term for the extermination of Jews. Literally, final solution.
Freikorps	Paramilitary units established by German veterans after WWI.
General Government	Part of Poland occupied by Germany in 1939 instead of being annexed and placed under German civil rule.
Gerichtsherr	In the SS and *Wehrmacht* the person taking the final decision of criminal prosecution of a lower-ranking functionary or soldier and whose permission is mandatory for confirming a sentence. Usually a division commander or the chief of a main SS office. In theory, Hitler was the highest *Gerichtsherr*.
Gestapo	Short for *Geheime Staatspolizei*, the German secret or political police, tasked with, among other things, prosecuting political opponents and Jews.
Hauptamt SS-Gericht	Main office of the SS responsible for judicial issues, including justice by SS- and police courts.
Holocaust	Name given after the war to the extermination of European Jews by the Nazi regime. After the Greek word *holokauston* (burned completely). Also called Shoah or Shoa, the Hebrew word for disaster or catastrophe.
HSSPF	Short for *Höhere SS- und Polizeiführer*. The highest representative of the SS and police in districts in Germany and in occupied territory. Smaller districts were supervised by an *SS- und Polizeiführer* (SSPF), the larger ones by the *Höchste SS- und Polizeiführer* (HöSSPF).
Kapo	Concentration camp inmate appointed by the camp staff to supervise fellow prisoners.

Kripo	Short for *Kriminalpolizei*, the German criminal investigation branch of the police.
NSDAP	National Sozialistische Deutsche Arbeiter Partei, Adolf Hitler's political party.
Orpo	Short for *Ordnungspolizei*, the uniformed police of Nazi Germany.
Rapportenführer	Member of the camp staff of the SS, responsible, among other things, for the regular counting of the prisoners.
Reichsarzt-SS	Chief of all physicians and medical personnel serving in the SS, including camp doctors. Responsible for medical issues within the organization, such as medical experiments in the concentration camps.
Reichsführer-SS	In short, RFSS. Highest rank within the SS, meant for the leader of the organization. From 1929 to 29 April 1945 this was Heinrich Himmler.
RSHA	Short for *Reichssicherheitshauptamt*, or Main Office of State Security, consisting of the Gestapo, *Kriminalpolizei*, *Grenzpolizei* and *Sicherheitsdienst*. In charge of prosecuting political opponents, fighting opposing groups and the extermination of Jews.
SA	Short for *Sturmabteilung*, the paramilitary branch of the Nazi party. Had after 1934 only propagandistic value. Members were known as brownshirts, after the colour of their uniform.
Schutzhaftlagerführer	Major member of camp staff, just below camp commander. Supervised the *Schutzhaftlager*, the part of each camp housing inmates. The superior of the *Rapportenführer* and *Blockführer*.
SD	Short for *Sicherheitsdienst*, the intelligence service of the SS.
Sipo	Short for *Sicherheitspolizei*, consisting of the *Gestapo* and *Kriminalpolizei*.
Sonderkommando	Literally, special unit. Name of various types of formations of the SS, for instance units of the *Einsatzgruppen*. Also the name for the teams of Jewish prisoners in the extermination camps responsible for the clearing of the gas chambers and running the crematories.
Spruchkammer	Courts established in Germany after the war conducting denazification trials from 1946 onwards. These courts grouped defendants in five categories: *Hauptschuldige* (prime suspects), *Belastete* (suspects), *Minderbelastete* (lesser suspects), *Mitläufer* (fellow travellers) and *Nichtbelastete* (innocents).
SS	Short for *Schutzstaffel*. National Socialist organization established as personal guard of Adolf Hitler which evolved to a state inside the state. Primarily responsible for police and security services.
SS- und Polizeigericht	Regional courts of the SS and police, responsible for the prosecution of police officers and SS members.
SSPF	See HSSPF.
SS-WVHA	*SS-Wirtschaft und Verwaltungshauptamt*, SS head office for economics and management. Responsible for administration,

	finances and building projects of the SS. The concentration camps were subordinate to this office, like the commercial enterprises of the SS in the field of agriculture, mining and weapons production.
SS-Totenkopfverbände	Death head units. Charged with security and management of the concentration camps.
Volksgerichthof	People's Court. Established by the Nazi regime in 1934, responsible for political transgressions such as high treason, defeatism and black market activities.
Waffen-SS	Military branch of the SS deployed at the front along with the *Wehrmacht*.
Wehrmacht	Armed forces of Nazi Germany, consisting of the Heer (land forces), Luftwaffe (air force) and Kriegsmarine (navy).

SS-ranks

SS-ranks:	British equivalent:
Reichsführer-SS	Field Marshal
SS-Oberstgruppenführer	General
SS-Obergruppenführer	Lieutenant General
SS-Gruppenführer	Major General
SS-Brigadeführer	Brigadier
SS-Oberführer	None
SS-Standartenführer	Colonel
SS-Obersturmbannführer	Lieutenant Colonel
SS-Sturmbannführer	Major
SS-Hauptsturmführer	Captain
SS-Obersturmführer	Lieutenant
SS-Untersturmführer	Second Lieutenant
SS-Sturmscharführer	Regimental Sergeant Major
SS-Hauptscharführer	(Company) Sergeant Major
SS-Oberscharführer	Staff Sergeant
SS-Scharführer	Sergeant
SS-Unterscharführer	Corporal
SS-Rottenführer	Lance Corporal
SS-Sturmmann	Senior Private
SS-Oberschütze	None
SS-Schütze	Private

The highest rank attained by Konrad Morgen was *SS–Sturmbannführer* (major).

Sources

Archives:
Das Bundesarchiv.
Franklin D. Roosevelt Library.
Harvard Law School Library.
Hessisches Hauptstaatsarchiv.
Landesarchiv Baden-Württemberg.
Standesamt Stadt Frankfurt am Main.
The Auschwitz-Birkenau State Museum.
US National Archives and Record Administration Washington.
Yale Law School Library.

Books:
Allen, M.T., *The Business of Genocide*, UNC Press Books, Chapel Hill (North Carolina, USA) 2002.
Arad, Y., *Belzec, Sobibor, Treblinka: The Operation Reinhard Death Camps*, Indiana University Press, Bloomington (Indiana, USA), 1999.
Bloxham, D., *Genocide on Trial*, Oxford University Press, Oxford, 2003.
Breitman, R., *Heinrich Himmler, de architect van de Holocaust*, Verbum, Laren, 2005.
Crowe, D.M., *Oskar Schindler*, Verbum, Laren, 2006.
Dederichs, M.R., *Heydrich: het gezicht van het kwaad*, Fontaine Uitgevers, 's Graveland, 2007.
Evans, R.J., *Het Derde Rijk Deel 1: Opkomst*, Spectrum, Utrecht, 2003.
Evans, R.J., *Het Derde Rijk Deel 2: Dictatuur*, Spectrum, Utrecht, 2006.
Evans, R.J., *Het Derde Rijk Deel 3: Oorlog*, Spectrum, Utrecht, 2009.
Fest, J., *De ondergang*, De Bezige Bij, Amsterdam, 2004.
Friedländer, H., *The Origins of Nazi Genocide: From Euthanasia to the Final Solution*, UNC Press Books, Chapel Hill (North Carolina), 1997.
Friedländer, S., *Nazi-Duitsland en de Joden*, Nieuw Amsterdam, 2007.
Gilbert, M., *The Routledge Atlas of the Holocaust*, Routledge, London, 2002.
Goldensohn, L., *Neurenberg gesprekken*, J.M. Meulenhoff, Amsterdam, 2004.
Hilberg, R., *De vernietiging van de Europese Joden*, Verbum, Laren, 2008.
Höhne, H., *Het zwarte korps onder de doodskop*, In den Toren, Baarn, 1983.
Holmes, R., *De wereld in oorlog*, De Boekerij, Amsterdam, 2008.
Höss, R. & Broad, P., Kremer, J.P., *KL Auschwitz seen by the SS*, The Auschwitz-Birkenau State Museum, Oświęcim, 2002.
Höss, R., *Commandant van Auschwitz: Zelfportret van een Beul*, Kruseman, Den Haag, 1960.
Jeffreys, D., *Het kartel van de hel*, De Bezige Bij, Amsterdam, 2009.
Kershaw, I., *Hitler, de Duitsers en de Holocaust*, Spectrum, Utrecht, 2009.
Kershaw, I., *Hitler: Hoogmoed 1889–1936*, Spectrum, Utrecht, 2003.

Kershaw, I., *Hitler: Vergelding 1936–1945*, Spectrum, Utrecht, 2003.

Klee, E., Dressen, W. & Riess, V., *'The good old days': The Holocaust as seen by its Perpetrators and Bystanders*, Konecky & Konecky, New York, 1988.

Klee, E., *Das Personenlexikon zum Dritten Reich*, Fischer, Frankfurt am Main, 2007.

Knopp, G., *Hitlers beulen*, De Prom, Baarn, 2001.

Knopp, G., *Hitlers Holocaust*, Byblos, Amsterdam, 2001.

Knopp, G., *Hitlers moordenaars*, Spectrum, Utrecht, 2004.

Kogon, E., *De SS-Staat*, Amsterdam Boek, Amsterdam, 1976.

Koszyk, K., *Pressepolitik und Propaganda im Ersten Weltkrieg*, Artemis Verlag, München, 1975.

Langbein, H., *People in Auschwitz*, UNC Press Books, Chapel Hill (North Carolina), 2004.

Levi, P., *Is dit een mens*, J.M. Meulenhoff, Amsterdam, 2004.

Longerich, P., *Heinrich Himmler*, De Bezige Bij, Amsterdam, 2009.

Longerich, P., *Holocaust: The Nazi Persecution and Murder of the Jews*, Oxford University Press, Oxford, 2010.

MacLean, F.L., *The Camp Men*, Schiffer Military History, Atglen (Pennsylvania), 1999.

Marcuse, H., *Legacies of Dachau: The Uses and Abuses of a Concentration Camp 1933–2001*, Cambridge University Press, Cambridge, 2001.

Morgen, K., *Kriegspropaganda und Kriegsverhütung*, Noske, Leipzig, 1936.

Olink, H., *Vrouwen van Vught*, Uitgeverij Bas Lubberhuizen, 's Hertogenbosch, 1995.

Overy, R., *Kroniek van het Derde Rijk*, De Bezige Bij, Amsterdam, 2011.

Overy, R., *The Penguin Historical Atlas of the Third Reich*, Penguin, London, 1996.

Pauer-Studer, H. & Velleman, J.D., *Konrad Morgen: The Conscience of a Nazi Judge*, Palgrave Macmillan, Hampshire, 2015.

Pelt, R.J. van & Dwork, D., *Auschwitz van 1270 tot heden*, Boom, Amsterdam, 1997.

Pendas, D.O., *The Frankfurt Auschwitz trial, 1963–1965*, Cambridge University Press, New York, 2006.

Pohl, D., *Holocaust*, Verbum, Laren, 2005.

Read, A., *Discipelen van de duivel*, Balans, Amsterdam, 2004.

Rees, L., *Auschwitz*, Anthos Manteau, Amsterdam, 2005.

Rees, L., *De nazi's*, Anthos Manteau, Amsterdam, 2007.

Roseman, M., *De villa Het meer De Conferentie*, Balans, Amsterdam, 2002.

Schelvis, J., *Ooggetuigen van Sobibor*, Ambo, Amsterdam, 2010.

Sereny, G., *De duisternis tegemoet*, Manteau, Den Haag, 1975.

Smith, L., *Vergeten stemmen van de Holocaust*, De Boekerij, Amsterdam, 2006.

Snyder, L.L., *Encyclopedia of the Third Reich*, Wordsworth, Hertfordshire (UK), 1998.

Snyder, T., *Bloedlanden*, Ambo, Amsterdam, 2011.

Spector, S. & Rozett, R., *Encyclopedie van de Holocaust*, Kok, Kampen, 2004.

Stackelberg, R. & Winkle, S.A., *The Nazi Germany Sourcebook*, Abingdon (Oxfordshire, UK), 2005.

Stafford, D., *Eindspel 1945*, Mouria, Amsterdam, 2008.

Stein, H., *Buchenwald concentration camp*, Wallstein, Frankfurt am Main, 2004.

Toland, J., *Adolf Hitler*, A.W. Bruna & Zoon, Utrecht, 1977.

Uijland, M. & Tijenk, C., *Eindpunt of tussenstation: Gids Nationaal Monument Kamp Vught*, Stichting Nationaal Monument Vught, 2002.

Veen, H. van der, *Westerbork 1939–1945*, Herinneringscentrum Kamp Westerbork, Hooghalen, 2003.

Vrba, R., *Ik ontsnapte uit Auschwitz*, Kok, Kampen, 2006.

Wachsmann, N., *KL: een geschiedenis van de naziconcentratiekampen*, De Bezige Bij, Amsterdam, 2015.
Walters, G., *De jacht op het kwaad*, Spectrum, Amsterdam, 2010.
Wiesel, E., *Nacht*, J.M. Meulenhoff, Amsterdam, 2006.
Wistrich, R.S., *Who's who in Nazi Germany*, Routledge, London, 2002.
Wittmann, R., *Beyond justice*, Harvard University Press, Cambridge (Massachusetts), 2005.
Yerger, M.C., *Allgemeine-SS*, Schiffer Military History, Atglen (Pennsylvania), 1997.

Articles:
'Ilse Koch, Lady mit Lampenschirm', *Der Spiegel*, nr. 7, 16.02.1950.
'West Germany: The Monster', *Time Magazine*, 14-07-1958.
Lindner, P., 'Überlebte Hermann Florstedt den Zweiten Weltkrieg?', *Zeitschrift für Heimatforschung*, 10, 2001.
Wehner, B., 'Das Spiel ist Aus – Arthur Nebe Glanz und Elend der Deutschen Kriminalpolizei', *Der Spiegel*, nr. 8, 23-02-1950.
Weingartner, J.J., 'Law and Justice in the Nazi SS: The Case of Konrad Morgen', *Central European History*, vol. 16, nr. 3, September 1983.

Online news articles:
Hinke, B., 'Demjanjuk vijf jaar de cel in voor wandaden in kamp Sobibor', *NRC*, 12-05-2011, op: www.nrc.nl/nieuws/2011/05/12/demjanjuk-vijf-jaar-de-cel-in-voor-wandaden-in-kamp-sobibor/
Kulke, U., 'Wie Hitler die Idee mit der Autobahn klaute', *Welt Geschichte*, 18-05-2015, op: www.welt.de/geschichte/zweiter-weltkrieg/article141052573/Wie-Hitler-die-Idee-mit-der-Autobahn-klaute.html
Nössig, F., 'Oberschloss Kranichfeld: Schlichte, wehrhafte Residenz', Thüringische Landeszeitung, 06-02-2011, op: www.tlz.de/web/zgt/kultur/detail/-/specific/Oberschloss-Kranichfeld-Schlichte-wehrhafte-Residenz-807305205

Websites:
avalon.law.yale.edu/subject_menus/imt.asp
axishistory.com
buchenwald.de
buchenwald.nl
dhm.de
forum.axishistory.com
holocaustresearchproject.org
jewishvirtuallibrary.org
justiz.bayern.de/gericht/olg/n/bauwerk
kz-gedenkstaette-dachau.de
loc.gov/rr/frd/Military_Law/Nuremberg_trials.html
nizkor.org
ns-archiv.de
nuremberg.law.harvard.edu
saalbau.com/auschwitz-prozess
tracesofwar.com
ushmm.org
www1.jur.uva.nl/junsv
yadvashem.org

Index